Bible Study
for Young Adults

FAITH

Living a Spiritual Life

Clifton F. Guthrie

Abingdon Press
Nashville

Faith: Living a Spiritual Life

20/30: Bible Study for Young Adults

by Clifton F. Guthrie

Copyright © 1999 by Abingdon Press

ISBN 0-687-08309-5

This book is printed on acid-free paper.

Manufactured in the United States of America.

04 05 06 07 08—10 9 8 7

CONTENTS

MEET THE WRITER

CLIFTON F. GUTHRIE is Assistant Professor of Homiletics and Pastoral Studies at Bangor Theological Seminary in Bangor, Maine. He currently serves as the co-editor of *Doxology: A Journal of Worship*.

Cliff has extensive teaching background at Candler School of Theology as well, having taught courses on systematic theology, preaching, United Methodist history, and worship and spirituality. His writing and editing credits include *For All the Saints: A Calendar of Commemorations for United Methodists* and numerous reviews and articles on the Christian calendar, pastoral care and practice, and worship issues. Cliff has offered papers and presentations at various academic society events.

Cliff has previously served as a local church pastor and youth minister and as an editor at The United Methodist Publishing House. He and his family reside in Bangor, Maine.

WELCOME TO 20/30: BIBLE STUDY FOR YOUNG ADULTS

The *20/30* Bible Study series is offered for post-modern adults who want to participate in and help structure their own discoveries—in life, in relationships, in faith. In each of the volumes of this series, participants will have the opportunity to use their own experience in life and faith to examine the biblical texts in new ways. You will examine biblical images that shape each person's life, including yours, even if we (or you) are not immediately aware that they do.

Image Is Everything

Images are what shape our decisions. We may think or know certain important data that weigh heavily in a decision. We may value the advice and counsel of others. We may find that the stated or implied wishes of others influence what we do. But in the end, it is often the *image* we hold that makes the decision.

For example, perhaps you were deeply hurt by someone important to you—an employer, a friend, even a pastor. You know in your heart that the institution is not to blame or that friendships are based on more than one event. But the image shaped by the difficult experience is that the job, or the friend, or the church cannot be relied upon. You *know* better, but you just have to make a change anyway. The image was more powerful than the reason.

Images are powerful, and they are familiar. In each of the studies in this series, you will encounter a well-known image that will connect your familiar experiences with some basis in Scripture.

You have faith, but may also realize that it can mean many things. Is it belief or trust or waiting or moral behavior or something else? Or it is all those things? *Faith: Living a Spiritual Life* helps you examine your faith and grow as a Christian.

You know what it's like to make agreements, to establish commitments, to give your word and expect to be trusted. *Covenant: Making Commitments That Count* engages you in study sessions that explain a variety of covenants, what happens when covenants are broken, how to have a faithful covenant to care for others and for the earth, and certainly, what it means to have this sacred covenant with God.

You know what it is like to move to a new place, to have to deal with transitions in school or work or in relationships. You have probably experienced changes in your family as you have grown up and moved out on your own. Some of these moves are gradual, just taken in stride. Others can be painful or abrupt; certainly life-changing. In *Exodus: Leaving Behind, Moving On*, you will appreciate learning how God is in the midst of those movements, no matter how minor or how transformational.

You know how important it is to have a sense of support and roots; to have friends and a life partner. *Community: Living Faithfully With Others* introduces you to Scriptures and life examples that delve into intimacy, work, family relationships, and more.

Experience, Faith, Growth, and Action

Each volume in this series will help you probe, on your own terms, how your experience links with your faith and how deepening your faith develops your life experience. If you need a prompt for your reflection, each volume has several pages of real life case studies. As your faith and commitment to Jesus Christ grow, you may be looking for ways to be involved in specific service opportunities. Several are listed on page 79.

We hope this series will help you encounter God through Scripture, reflection, and dialogue with others who desire to grow in faith and to serve others. One image we hold is that God is in all things. God is certainly with you.

HOW TO USE
THIS RESOURCE

Each session of this resource includes similar components or elements:
- a statement of the issue or question to be explored;
- several "voices" of persons who are currently dealing with that issue;
- exploration of biblical passages relative to the question raised;
- "Bible 101" boxes that provide insight about the study of the Bible;
- questions for reflection and discussion;
- suggested individual and group activities designed to bring the session to life;
- optional case studies (found in the back of the book);
- various service learning activities related to the session (found in the back of the book).

Choices, Choices, Choices

Collectively, these components mean one thing: *choice*. You have choices to make concerning how to use each session of this resource. Want just the nitty-gritty Bible reading, reflection, and study for personal or group use? Then focus your attention on just those components during your study time.

Like starting with real-life stories about issues then moving into how the Bible might be relevant? Start with the "voices" and move on from there. Use the "voices" to encourage group members to speak about their own experiences.

Prefer highly charged discussion encounters where many different viewpoints can be heard? Start the session with the biblical passages, followed by the questions and group activities. Be sure to compare the ideas found in the "Bible 101" boxes with your current ideas for more discussion. Want the major challenge of applying biblical principles to a difficult problem? After reading the biblical material, read one of the case studies, using the guidelines provided on page 14 or get involved with one of the service learning options described on 79.

Great Versatility

This resource has been designed for many different uses. Some persons will use this resource for personal study and reflection. Others will want to explore the work with a small group of friends. And still other folks will see this book as a different type of Sunday school resource.

Spend some time thinking about your own questions, study habits, and learning styles or those of your small group. Then use the guidelines mentioned above to fashion each session into a unique Bible study session to meet those requirements.

Highly Participatory

As you will see, the Scriptures, "voices," commentary, and experience of group members will provide an opportunity for an active, engaging time together. The greatest challenge for a group leader might be "crowd control"—being sure everyone has the chance to put his or her ideas into the mix!

The Scriptures will help you and those who study with you to make connections between real-life issues and the Bible. This resource values and encourages personal participation as a means to fully understand and appreciate the intersection of personal belief with God's ongoing work in each and every life.

ON ORGANIZING A SMALL GROUP

Learning with a small group of persons offers certain advantages over studying by yourself. First, you will hopefully encounter different opinions and ideas, making the experience of Bible study a richer and more challenging event. Second, any leadership responsibilities can be shared among group members. Third, different persons will bring different talents. Some will be deep thinkers while other group members will be creative giants. Some persons will be newcomers to the Bible; their questions and comments will help others clarify their deeply held assumptions.

So how does one go about forming a small group? Follow the steps below and see how easy this task can be.

■ **Read through the resource carefully.** Think about the ideas presented, the questions raised, and the exercises suggested. If the sessions of this work excite you, it will be easier for you to share your enthusiasm to others.

■ **Spend some time thinking about church members, friends, and co-workers who might find the sessions of this resource interesting.** On a sheet of paper, write down two characteristics or talents you see in each person that would make them an attractive Bible study group member. Some talents might include "deep thinker," "creative wizard," or "committed Christian." Remember: the best small group has members who differ in learning styles, talents, ideas, and convictions, but who respect the dignity and integrity of the other members.

■ **Most functional small groups have 7-15 members.** Make a list of potential group members that doubles your target number. For instance, if you would like a small group of seven to ten members, be prepared to invite fourteen to twenty persons.

■ **Once your list of potential candidates is complete, decide on a tentative location and time.** Of course, the details can be negotiated with those persons who accept the invitation, but you need to sound definitive and clear to prospective group members. "We will initially set Wednesday night from 7-9 P.M. at my house for our meeting time" will sound more attractive than "Well, I don't know either when or where we would be meeting, but I hope you will consider joining us."

- **Make initial contact with prospective group members short, sweet, and to the point.** Say something like, "We are putting together a Bible study using a different kind of resource. When would be a good time to show you the resource and talk about the study?" Establishing a special time to make the invitation takes the pressure off the prospective group member to make a quick decision.

- **Show up at the decided time and place.** Talk with each prospective member individually. Bring a copy of the resource with you. Show them what excites you about the study and mention the two unique characteristics or talents you feel they would offer the group. Tell them the initial meeting time and location and how many weeks the small group will meet. Also mention that the need for a new time or location could be discussed during the first group meeting. Ask for a commitment to come to the first session. Thank them for their time.

- **Give a quick phone call or email to thank all persons for their consideration and interest.** Remind persons of the time and location of the first meeting.

- **Be organized.** Use the first group meeting to get acquainted. Briefly describe the seven sessions. Have a book for each group member and discuss sharing responsibilities for leadership.

LEADING AND SHARING LEADERSHIP

So the responsibility to lead the group has fallen on you? Don't sweat it. Follow these simple suggestions and you will razzle and dazzle the group with your expertise.

- **Read the session carefully.** Look up all the Bible passages. Take careful notes about the ideas, statements, questions, and activities in the session. Try all the activities.

- **Using 20-25 blank index cards, write one idea, activity, Bible passage, or question from the session on each card** until you either run out of material or cards. Be sure to look at the case studies and service learning options. Number the cards so they will follow the order of the session.

- **Spend a few moments thinking about the members of your group.** How many like to think about ideas, concepts, or problems? How many need to "feel into" an idea by storytelling, worship, prayer, or group activities? Who are the "actors" who prefer a hands-on or participatory approach, such as an art project or simulation, to grasp an idea? Write down the names of all group members and record whether you believe them to be a THINKER, FEELER, or an ACTOR.

- **Place all the index cards in front of you in the order in which they originally appeared in the session.** Looking at that order, ask yourself: (1) Where is the "Head" of the session—the key ideas or concepts? (2) Where is the "Heart" of the session in which persons will have a deep feeling response? (3) Where are the "Feet"—those activities that ask the group to put the ideas and feelings to use? Separate the cards into three stacks: HEAD, HEART, and FEET.

- **Now construct the "body" for your class.** Shift the cards around, using a balance of HEAD, HEART, and FEET cards to determine which activities you will do and in what order. This will be your group's unique lesson plan. Try to choose as many cards as you have group members. Then, match the cards: HEAD and THINKERS; HEART and FEELERS; FEET and ACTORS for each member of the group. Don't forget a card for yourself. For instance, if your group has ten members, you should have about ten cards.

- **Develop the leadership plan.** Invite these group members prior to the session to assist in the leadership. Show them the unique lesson plan you developed. Ask for their assistance in developing and/or leading each segment of the session as well as a cool introduction and a closing ritual or worship experience.

Your lesson plan should start with welcoming the participants. Hopefully everyone will have read the session ahead of time. Then, begin to move through the activity cards in the order of your unique session plan, sharing the leadership as you have agreed.

You may have chosen to have all the HEAD cards together, followed by the HEART cards. This would introduce the session's content, followed by helping group members "feel into" the issue through interactive stories, questions, and exercises with all group members. Feel free to add more storytelling, discussion, prayer, mediation, or worship.

You may have chosen to use the FEET cards to end the session. Ask the group, "What difference should this session make in our daily lives?" You or the ACTORS should introduce the FEET cards as possible ways to discern a response. Ensuring that group members leave with a few practical suggestions for doing something different during the week is the point of this section of the unique lesson plan.

- **Remember: leading the group does not mean "Do it all yourself."** With a little planning, you can enlist the talents of many group members. By inviting group members to lead parts of the session that feel comfortable for them, you will model and encourage shared leadership. Welcome their interests in music, prayer, worship, Bible, and so on, to develop innovative and creative Bible study sessions that can transform lives in the name of Jesus Christ.

CHOOSING TEACHING OPTIONS

This young adult series was designed, written, and produced out of an understanding of the attributes, concerns, joys, and faith issues of young adults. With great care and integrity, this image-based print resource was developed to connect biblical events and relationships with contemporary, real-life situations of young adults. Its pages will promote Christian relationships and community, support new biblical learning, encourage spiritual development, and empower faithful decision-making and action.

This study is well-suited to young adults and may be used confidently and effectively. But with the great diversity within the young adult population, not every line of this study will be written "just for you." To be most relevant, some portions of the study material need to be tailored to fit your particular group. Adjustments for a good fit involve making choices from options offered by the resource. This customizing may be done easily by a designated leader who is familiar with the layout of the resource and the young adults who are using it.

What to Expect

In this study, Scripture and real-life images mesh together to provoke a personal response. Young adults will find themselves thinking, feeling, imagining, questioning, making decisions, professing faith, building connections, inviting discipleship, taking action, and making a difference. Scripture is at the core of each session. Scenarios weave in the dimensions of real life. Narrative and text boxes frame plenty of teaching options to offer young adults.

Each session is part of a cohesive volume, but is designed to stand alone. One session is not dependent on knowledge or experience accumulated from other sessions. A group leader can freely choose from the teaching options in an individual session without wondering about how it might affect the other sessions.

A Good Fit

For a better fit, alter the session based on what is known about the young adult participants. Young adults are a diverse constituency with varied experiences, interests, needs, and values. There is really no single defining characteristic that links young adults. Specific information about the age, employment status, household, personal relationships, and lifestyle among participants will equip a leader to make choices that ensure a good fit.

- **Customize.** Read through the session. Notice how scenarios and teaching options move from integrating Scripture and real-life dimensions to inviting a response.

- **Look at the scenario(s).** How real is the presentation of real-life? Say that the main character is a professional, white male, married, in his late twenties and caught in a workplace dilemma that entangles his immediate superior and a subordinate from his division. Perhaps your group members are mostly college students and recent graduates, unmarried, and still on the way to being "settled." There are many differences between the man in the scenario and the group members using this resource.

As a leader, you could choose to eliminate the case study, substitute it with another scenario (there are several more choices on pages 75–78), claim the validity of the dilemma, and shift the spotlight from the main character to the subordinate, or modify the description of the main character. Break-Out groups based on age or employment experience might also be used to accommodate the differences and offer a better fit.

- **Look at the teaching options.** How are the activities propelling participants toward a personal response? Perhaps the Scripture study requires more meditative quiet than is possible and a more academic, verbal, or artistic approach would offer a better fit. Maybe more direct decisions or actions would fit better than more passive or logical means. Try to keep a balance, though, that allows participants to "get out of their head" to reflect and also to move toward action.

Conceivably, there could just be too much in any one session. As a leader, you can pick and choose among teaching options, substitute case studies, take two meetings to do one session, and adapt any process to make a better fit. The tailoring process can be evaluated as adjustments are made. Judge the fit every time you meet. Ask questions that gauge relevance and assess how the resource has stretched minds, encouraged discipleship, and changed lives.

USING BREAK-OUT GROUPS

20/30 Break-Out groups are small groups that encourage the personal sharing of lives and the gospel. The name "Break-Out" is a sweeping term that includes a variety of small group settings. A Break-Out group may resemble a Bible study group, an interest group, a sharing group, or other types of Christian fellowship groups.

Break-Out groups offer young adults a chance to belong and personally relate to one another. Members are known, nurtured, and heard by others. Young adults may agree and disagree while maximizing the exchange of ideas, information, or options. They might explore, confront, and resolve personal issues and feelings with empathy and support. Participants can challenge and hold each other accountable to a personalized faith and stretch its links to real-life and service.

Forming Break Out Groups

The nature of these small Break-Out groups will depend on the context and design of the specific session. On occasion the total group of participants will be divided for a particular activity. Break-Out groups will differ from one session to the next. Variations may involve the size of the group, how group members are divided, or the task of the group. Break-Out groups may also be used to accommodate differences and help tailor the session plan for a better fit. In some sessions, specific group assembly instructions will be provided. For other sessions, decisions regarding the size or division of small groups will be made by the designated leader. Break-Out groups may be in the form of pairs or trios, family-sized groups of 3-6 members, or groups of up to ten members.

They may be arranged simply by grouping persons seated next to each other or in more intentional ways by common interests, characteristics, or life experience. Consider creating Break-Out groups according to age; gender; type of household, living arrangements, or love relationships; vocation, occupation, career, or employment status; common or built-in connections; lifestyle; values or perspective; or personal interests or traits.

Membership

The membership of Break-Out groups will vary from session to session, or even within specific sessions. Young adults need to work at knowing and being known, so that there can be a balance between Break-Out groups that are more similar and those that reflect greater diversity. There may be times when more honest communication, trust, or accountability may be desired and group leaders will need to be free to self-select small group members.

It is important for *20/30* Break-Out groups to practice acceptance and to value the worth of others. The potential for small groups to encourage personal sharing and significant relationships is enhanced when members agree to exercise active listening skills, keep confidences, expect authenticity, foster trust, and develop ways of loving one another. All group members contribute to the development and function of Break-Out groups. Designated leaders especially need to model manners of hospitality and help ensure that each group member is respected.

Invitational Listening

Consider establishing an "invitational listening" routine that validates the perspective and affirms the voice of each group member. After a question or statement is posed, pause and allow time to think—not everyone thinks on their feet or talks out loud to think. Then, initiate conversation by inviting one group member, by name, to talk. This person may either choose to talk or to "pass." Either way, this person is honored and is offered an opportunity to speak and be heard. This person carries on the ritual by inviting another group member, by name, to speak. The process continues until all have been invited, by name, to talk. As each one invites another, the responsibility of acceptance and hospitality in the Break-Out groups is shared among all its members.

Study group members Break-Out to belong, to share the gospel, to care, and to watch over one another in Christian love. "So deeply do we care for you that we are determined to share with you not only the gospel of God but also our own selves, because you have become very dear to us" (1 Thessalonians 2:8).

FAITH:
LIVING A SPIRITUAL LIFE

- "I have faith in God, but I am not particularly religious. For me, to have faith is to act, to try to help others, and to make the world a more just and peaceful place, no matter how bleak things may sometimes be."
- "For me, having a faith is a matter of belonging to a community of shared values, beliefs, and rituals. I happen to be a member of the Christian faith, but there are many other faiths in the world."
- "Faith is a fundamental trust that I have in God. There are lots of things my church teaches that I may sometimes doubt, but in my heart I know that God exists and is actively involved in the world around me."
- "To have faith is to believe that what God tells us is true, particularly what God tells us in Scripture."
- "I think of faith as something very personal, in fact, I am probably more comfortable talking about my sex life than my faith. Everyone is on his or her own journey."

It is obvious that the word *faith* is used in different ways. For some, faith is primarily a matter of the body, something you do. For others, faith is more a matter of the heart, something you feel. Still others think of it as a set of beliefs, something that is primarily a matter of the head. Each of these understandings of faith is biblical; that is, they can all be found somewhere in the collection of writings that make up the Bible.

Part of what we will do in *Faith: Living a Spiritual Life* is to explore all these options and others. The realization that the Bible speaks of faith in many ways may be very liberating to you if you have grown up in a church that has spoken of it in only one way. If your definition of faith is certain to you, it could be a bit unsettling.

Despite the wide range of biblical understandings of faith, it will become clear as you move through these sessions that the Bible does not think that the question of faith is unimportant. Neither is it comfortable with the attitude that anything you happen to think about it is okay. Through over one hundred generations of trial and error, Christians have come to believe that there are some understandings of faith that are central to being in relationship with the God spoken of in the Bible and revealed in Jesus of Nazareth. There are other ways of understanding faith that are less important or even misguided or harmful.

So if you are of the opinion that everyone is "entitled to their opinion" on the matter of faith, you may experience this study's insistence that some opinions are better than others as hopelessly narrow or old-fashioned.

However you come to this study, alone or in a group, certain or uncertain, dragged kicking and screaming or eager to learn all you can, you are welcome. You are invited to engage in this study with an open mind and an open heart. You are encouraged to be honest with yourself and one another. The one option we hope you won't choose is to remain aloof and unaffected. The question of our faith goes to the heart of the meaning of our lives. And this is not a subject that most people find unimportant.

More people than ever are trying to broaden their spiritual horizons. They want to find out about this thing called faith and see how they can incorporate it into their daily lives. No one operates without a certain set of beliefs. Yet, beliefs may differ vastly among individuals, families, and communities. As we explore in these sessions, having beliefs about God is not always the same thing as having faith in God, nor acting as faithful persons in the presence of God.

As technology continues to remake our world into a global community, our beliefs about God, religion, and everything else will be filtered through a lens of awareness of other peoples, lands, and religious customs. So our study of faith inevitably faces a dual question: How can we participate in a vigorous, even life-changing, study of the depth of our particular faith without becoming bad neighbors to those in our world community who believe differently? On the other hand, how can we avoid the other danger of so valuing the diversity of belief that we end up believing everything and therefore nothing much at all?

Being faithful Christians in our day and age means that we cannot pretend that other religions either don't exist or are without worth. Neither can we expect to practice "religion in general" and hope to make any real progress in the life of faith. We study the Bible because we hope to be better Christians and therefore be better people. The truth of Christianity can never be proven by its popularity among or superiority over the world's many other religions. Its truth can only ever be an experience of the transformed lives of those who follow Christ.

And we are hungry for such transformation. The dramatic explosions in information, communications, entertainment, and consumer choices, not to mention the challenges of world poverty, pollution, and prejudice, make the human spiritual quest more daunting than ever. In the middle of this noise, this cacophony of challenges, choices, and crises, the call of Jesus seems ever more important and persistent: "Come to me, all you that are weary and are carrying heavy burdens, and I will give you rest. Take my yoke upon you, and learn from me; for I am gentle and humble in heart, and you will find rest for your souls. For my yoke is easy, and my burden is light" (Matthew 11:28-30).

FAITH AND BELIEF

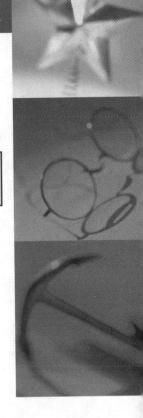

> This session examines the relationship between faith and belief.

A TIME OF CHANGE

What does it mean to have faith? to have faith in God? What is the relationship between faith and belief?

As we grow older and gain experience in the real world, many of the things we believed when we were younger begin to change or even to drop away. When this happens to our religious belief, it can be confusing and painful. It can also be exciting.

By the time we are young adults, most of us have attended churches or even experimented with faiths different than the tradition in which we were raised. Some of us are coming back to Christianity after a long absence, seeking to deepen our spirituality or to renew our ties with a church for the sake of our children. Others of us never really left, but never really engaged in our faith in an intentional, personal way either. For all of us, faith and belief are dynamic, changing experiences, not packages of heavenly truths that we inherited from our parents and accepted without question.

START

A Time of Change
Getting Started

Introduce yourselves to one another or check in with one another if your group is already well acquainted. Giving a moment or two to reflect on your answers, have everyone in the group name two things: (1) something you believed when you were a young child but later found out not to be true; and
(2) something that you are not sure whether you believe but hope is true.

Alternative: Read the five statements about faith found at the beginning of the Introduction on page 17. Which ones do you feel are most in tune with your own understanding of the meaning of "faith"? Which ones are most alien to you? Why?

STRANGE LANGUAGE

Even the regular churchgoer cannot help but be disoriented by the difference between the language of everyday life and church talk. Christians speak and sing of things on Sunday morning that sound very strange to our modern ears: martyrs, miracles, angels, virgins, sin, sacrifice, and salvation.

How do we know what all these things mean and which of them are essential to a life of faith? To what are we willing to give our assent? What kind of God can I have faith in? And does this God matter to me? care for me? What if I don't know what I really believe?

The Apostles' Creed

The Apostles' Creed was not actually written by Jesus' apostles, but emerged in the third and fourth centuries, probably in Rome, for use with adults who were getting baptized. It was a distillation of the beliefs that they were to hold (but not necessarily entirely understand!) as new Christians.

MEET DAVID AND TONYA

David is upset after receiving yet another job rejection letter. He is stuck in an entry-level position that does not take advantage of the skills and knowledge he gained at the university. He mentions the rejection to a co-worker, Tonya, who responds glibly, "I have faith that things will work out for you."

David: Why are you always that way? You can never empathize with anyone!

Tonya: Don't you have faith?

David: Of course, but it's not the same as

yours. You sometimes seem to live in a magical world, as if you believe that if you close your eyes and pray hard enough you can make anything happen.

Tonya: Well, I do believe that God answers our prayers. When my parents didn't have enough money to send me to college, I prayed fervently for a scholarship. The next month, one of the colleges I applied to offered me a full scholarship. God answered my prayer precisely as I had prayed it.

David: You make God sound like Santa Claus. I don't believe that God rearranges the world to suit peoples' needs just because they pray hard. If that were true, the world wouldn't be filled with poverty and illness. If I get a new job, it will be a result of hard work and good contacts.

Tonya: Then what is the use of this faith you claim you have?

David: To me, faith is more a matter of engaging life purposefully and helping others than believing impossible things. God wants to use us to make the world a better place, not wait around for blessings from beyond.

Tonya: My God is more personal than that. We talk about everything.

I(ŊPOSSIBLE THINGS

In *Through the Looking Glass*, the Queen of Hearts tells Alice to shut her eyes and try hard to believe that the queen is one hundred and one years old. But Alice objects that one cannot believe impossible things. The Queen says, "When I was your age, I always did it for half-an-hour a day. Why, sometimes I've believed as many as six impossible things before breakfast."

Too many people think of religion, and particularly Christianity, as a matter of having to believe impossible things. Faith

Meet David and Tonya
Read the dialogue between David and Tonya. Do you identify with one more than the other? In what way? Which of the following things would you feel comfortable praying to God for? Why?

- the health or healing of a person you care for
- to solve a personal financial problem
- world peace
- doing your best on an exam or interview
- finding your true lovematch
- finding a good parking space
- forgiveness
- good weather for a special occasion
- wisdom to know what is right and wrong
- strength to do the right thing

Impossible Things
- Which comes first, faith or belief? Why? How are the two related?
- Can you recall an instance when your beliefs became clearer once you made a personal investment in something?
- Faith and belief are strangely human things. As far as we know, no other animals on earth engage in religion or struggle with faith and belief. Why do you think our particular species finds it necessary to have religions? Would we survive as a species without faith? Why or why not?

Trees and Rock
Read Matthew 7:15-23. Jesus seems to divide persons into "good trees" and "bad trees." He also speaks of the exclusion of some persons from the "kingdom of heaven." What do you think it means to do things in the name of the Lord? Is it possible to act in God's name and not have that action favored by God? Explain.

Do you think God lets everyone into heaven? Are some excluded? Why or why not? On what basis are they considered good or bad, included or excluded?

SMALL GROUP

Review Matthew 7:24-28, the parable of the wise and foolish builder. Brainstorm a list of things that you look for when you buy a house (good foundation, good roof, plenty of room to grow, and so on). Write this list down on a chalkboard or a piece of poster paper. Next, think about the "house of faith" to which you belong. Come up with parallels between a solid house and your "house of faith." For example, the family room can signify the friendships you develop in church. Use your imagination.

Have you ever moved from one house of faith to another? What was more attractive to you about the new house? What is the best feature of the house you live in now? What home repairs are needed?

and belief are related, but they are not the same things. I can believe all kinds of things (dogs are better than cats, angels have wings and stand by my bed at night, or even God exists), that make little or no practical difference in how I actually live my life.

Faith, on the other hand, is a matter of personal investment. Faith usually implies belief, but it also assumes that this belief makes a profound difference in how I treat others, engage the world, or spend my time and money. Faith moves me to risk, sacrifice, grow, and challenge. Believing is easy; it requires nothing much of us. But having true faith is the hardest thing in the world. Interestingly, many people report that they don't really know what they believe until they begin to act on faith.

TREES AND ROCK

Read Matthew 7:15-29.

In this portion of what we now call the Sermon on the Mount, Jesus spoke directly to the difference between belief and faith. He cautioned those who dared to call themselves his followers: "Not everyone who says to me, 'Lord, Lord,' will enter the kingdom of heaven, but only the one who does the will of my Father in heaven" (7:21). His parable of the houses built on sand or rock is appropriate for the difference between building a spiritual life built on belief or faith. When the winds and rain of hard times come, a life built on belief alone has little substance to it. A life built on faith, however, can withstand the fury of the worst storms.

THINGS NOT SEEN

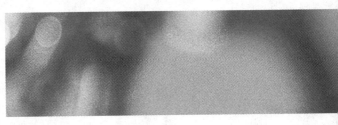

One of the classic definitions of faith in the Bible can be found in Hebrews 11:1: "Now faith is the assurance of things hoped for, the conviction of things not seen."

The Letter to the Hebrews is an extended essay in which the writer argues that the priesthood of Jesus is superior to the priesthood of the Temple in Jerusalem (Hebrews 4:14–5:6; 7:23–8:6). It is not easy for us to see what an outrageous claim this was—after all, the Temple had stood for centuries and was the center of Jewish faith and life. Here was a substantial building of stone and brick standing solidly on the top of a mountain in which a person could worship God with a gift or animal sacrifice. But this letter claims that the physical Temple, as solid as it seemed, was merely a "sketch and shadow" of a temple that was visible only to the eyes of faith. This is the heavenly temple where God actually dwells, and over which Jesus presides as high priest (8:5).

The first people to hear the words of this letter read were undergoing persecution for their Christian faith. They were probably feeling that God had abandoned them. They probably looked nostalgically on the certainty of God's presence that worship in the physical Temple provided.

But for the writer of Hebrews, faith is a matter of maintaining hope for the future in the face of present suffering. It is a matter of acting on "things not seen." To be told that their hope was not based on a temporal building made of brick (which in fact was utterly destroyed by the Romans in A.D.

Things Not Seen

Look more carefully at Hebrews 11:1 and its definition of faith. For what do you truly hope? For yourself, your family, your community, the world? Write down a list of these hopes. Are all these "hopes" equally important or valid? Which are most fundamental? Why?

Closer Look

Read Revelation 21 to see how another early Christian writer used the image of an entirely new Jerusalem coming down from heaven to give hope to another Christian community undergoing suffering and persecution. Interestingly, in the New Jerusalem, there would be no temple at all because God would dwell with the people directly (Revelation 22:22). How does this heavenly image enhance your faith?

70), but an eternal temple in God's heaven, must have been an immense encouragement to them.

FAITH FOR WHAT?

Read Hebrews 11:4-38.

Barbara Brown Taylor, an Episcopal priest, has said, "Faith, for me, is a dangling modifier. When people tell me that they have faith, I want to ask, Faith in what? Faith that *what* will happen?"

One can believe a lot of crazy things and still not have faith. Faith seems to be a question of what you do with what you believe.

After telling us that faith is a matter of acting on "things unseen," the writer of Hebrews gives us an astounding list of persons who had done just that: Cain, Noah, Abraham, Moses, Rahab. Each of them acted in their present time as if the future they hoped for *was already true*. By faith they took steps toward a life with God that may not have been visible, but was absolutely real—because it changed the way they acted.

So numerous are these people that they are called a "cloud of witnesses" (12:1). Imagine you are a part of that early community for which this letter was written, hearing this roll call of name after name read to you. That cloud would become your new reality, a reality upon which you yourself could step out in faith—just as the writer encourages: "Let us also lay aside every weight and the sin that clings so closely, and let us run with perseverance the race that is set before us" (12:1).

Imagine, the letter says, that the world that God wants to exist already does, and act on it. Imagine that God is near you, upholding you, surrounding you with

---

Faith for What?

- Go over the list of examples in Hebrews 11:4-38. Find the individual stories in a Bible dictionary, if necessary, or find the stories told in the Old Testament. Which of these intrigue you most? Why?

- If the Bible had been written today instead of two thousand years ago, what people might be included among this "cloud of witnesses"? Name one person in your life who has demonstrated their faith. How was this done?

- The question of "faith for what" is a good one. Take some time to imagine what the world would look like if the religion you espouse actually "won" or became the religion the whole world followed. What problems would be solved? What problems would remain?

witnesses, and act on it. Ask what it means to worship with your entire being in a temple that reaches into heaven—and act on it.

It cannot be touched. It is more real than that:

"You have not come to something that can be touched, a blazing fire, and darkness, and gloom, and a tempest, and the sound of a trumpet, and a voice whose words made the hearers beg that not another word be spoken to them. . . . But you have come to . . . the city of the living God, the heavenly Jerusalem, and to innumerable angels in festal gathering . . ." (12:18-19, 22).

A PRESENT ACT

Faith is a *present* act (something that you have or do now) that is oriented toward a future hope. It is a curious thing for a human being to have: it both assumes the reality of and actually brings into existence God's work in the world. Faith is an intangible that brings forth the tangible. Faith is similar to entering another dimension in time and space.

It is also a form of knowing. You see things hoped for happen before they materialize before the naked eye. With this kind of certainty many ordinary people have done extraordinary things. They become outstanding teachers, socially transforming lawyers, lifesaving doctors, and visionary political leaders.

A Present Act

- Can you think of a time when you had to act on faith? What for? What was the result?
- What does it mean to you that faith is a gift? How does one receive the gift of faith? Do you believe that this a once-for-all gift or something that you receive again and again?
- Is your faith growing? What are some of the biggest hindrances to your faith?

Fusing the Word With My World

How do we know God's love as a reality in our lives? Is it something we feel? a sensation of the gut? Is God's love a reality to you? What intimations of this love have you learned to trust? What place does love play in faith? What can cause us to doubt the reality of this love? What evidence do you see of God's love for the entire world? What evidence do you see for God's absence or disregard of the world? Which evidence is stronger? Why?

Even so, faith is not something that you get by gritting your teeth and trying really hard. This is perhaps the most difficult thing for us to understand in a culture that stresses self-reliance and independence. Yet Christians have always insisted that faith *is a gift from God*. It is a form of what they call "grace," an expression of God's love for us. We don't earn this love, we only awaken to its reality. Yet like any love, we are called to respond to it if it is to grow.

FUSING THE WORD WITH MY WORLD

Think about ways that you can respond to the love of God and grow your faith. Is there a fear that you need to overcome to move your life in a more positive direction? Is there something wrong happening in your family, church, or community that needs the attention of a courageous person? How can faith make your engagement with these things more than a matter of "just trying harder" or "believing impossible things?"

For many people, God's love is never more than a belief, something abstract. Those who are more fortunate know it as a reality; they know it by faith.

Closing

Light a candle if one is available. Close your eyes and think about a way that you need to step out in faith. Get a clear idea in your mind what that first step looks like. Plan a time and a way for you to take that first step.

As you imagine the future that might be, meditate on the following: "I can do all things through Christ who strengthens me" (Philippians 4:13).

Optional: As you close, invite each person to tell the group what step of faith they plan to take. Write these down and save them for next week.

CONFIDENCE

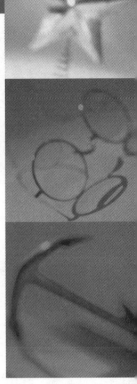

> This session explores two dimensions of confidence
> and asks how faith can center our lives.

NEW RESPONSIBILITIES

As young adults, most of us are experiencing an enormous increase in our responsibilities. Our age, skill, and experience introduce us to worlds that may have been closed to us before:

- home ownership
- supervisory responsibilities at work
- marriage
- graduate school
- children
- aging and sick parents
- new financial concerns like retirement accounts, life insurance, and self-employment taxes.

START

Getting Started

Check in with one another. If your group made a list of the steps of faith that you were planning this week, go around the room and ask people to report on what happened.

New Responsibilities

Read this section and then name some other new responsibilities that come to one's life as a twenty- or thirty- year-old adult. Have someone in the group list these on a chalkboard or piece of poster paper. Which of these responsibilities have been welcomed and exciting? Which ones have come to you even though you did not want them? What responsibilities not listed may be just around the corner for you?

FRESH ANXIETIES

Fresh Anxieties

Break into small groups. Think of a recent, major transition that you have experienced in your work, personal, or family life. Tell that to one another. What new anxieties or concerns accompanied this transition? Be specific. If the anxieties were resolved, tell how.

Each of these new responsibilities can bring fresh worries. Consider these cases:

- A new father readies a car seat to leave the hospital with his wife and their newborn baby. A voice inside asks, *Will I make a good parent? Will I avoid the mistakes and hurts my parents inflicted on me?*
- The graduate school student teaches her first class. She wonders, *When will they discover that I am an imposter and that I don't really know this material all that well?*
- A broken engagement leaves a twenty-four-year-old man shattered. He stares at his receding hairline in the mirror and wonders whether anyone will ever love him enough to marry him.
- The newly commissioned lieutenant is given her first command. Will the enlisted soldiers under her charge obey her orders?
- The young comic flubbs his lines. His routine falls to the stage floor and dies a slow and painful death. Sheer silence from the audience and another show in an hour. . . .

COMPETENCE AND WORTHINESS

Competence and Worthiness

Look back at the cases under "Fresh Anxieties" and consider similar situations you may have named in the group exercise for that section. Which of these anxieties are questions of *competence* and which are questions of *worthiness*? Are your own anxieties more one than the other? Explain.

In your experience or opinion, does religious faith primarily address one of these more than the other? Why? How does your faith address these two dimensions of confidence?

Psychologists have pointed out that self-esteem involves two major levels of self-questioning. The first is a question of *competence*: Am I smart enough (fast enough, skilled enough, and so on) to meet the challenge in front of me? The second is the question of *worthiness*: Am I an acceptable person? Do others love me? Do I love myself? When we ask this question in religious terms, it comes out, "Does God love me? Do I trust God enough to believe that God loves me?"

Each of us can probably name ways that we have questioned ourselves as we have faced new challenges. Our competence to do our work, relate to our families, or manage our finances is always before us. When faced with a new task, we commonly try to deal with it by gaining information or skill in that area of competence: we read a book on parenting, we search the Internet for help, or we enroll in a course at the local college.

Underneath these specific anxieties and solutions, however, there is that second level of self-worth and love: Do others like me? Do all of these new responsibilities add up to a meaningful life? Is the path that is unfolding before me really the direction I ought to be taking? Have I missed my "calling?" Does my spiritual life ground me and give me confidence? Does it undergird and bring into focus everything I do, or is it just one more part of my overly hectic life?

FAITH AS TRUST

In the collection of writings known as the Hebrew Bible, or to Christians as the Old Testament, the Hebrew word most commonly translated into English as faith is *emunah*, and suggests trust or firmness of mind. In the Old Testament, there is no equivalent to the English noun "faith." Rather, faith is always a verb. *Emunah* meant to be certain of something. Faith in God meant being confident of God's promises, commands, or power.

What are the qualities of a confident person? For the Hebrews, faith gave one a sense of stability in the face of change. The prophet Isaiah put it nicely: "One who trusts will not panic" (28:16). Later, in Isaiah 30:12-18, the prophet paints a sharp

Read Genesis 15:1-6 as a story that exemplifies the notion that faith is trust in God. Why do you think Abram trusted God—was it the vision or the content of the promise God made? Can you think of any other examples in the Bible where faith in God was primarily a matter of trust? List these.

SMALL GROUP

Faith as Trust

Place a chair somewhere in the room. Take turns trying to find and sit in the chair with your eyes closed or blindfolded, using only the verbal commands of the other group members to guide you. You are not allowed to reach out or touch the chair with any part of your body before you sit down.

After everyone who wants to has tried this, ask: How did it feel to follow the voice and direction of another? Were you tempted to use some other means (peeking, touching) to supplement the verbal commands you received? Will anyone admit to cheating? Did you believe that they were instructing you correctly? Did you feel sure that the chair would be there and it would hold you? How did it make you feel to sit without seeing?

Relate what just happened to having trust or confidence in God. What are the differences? What are the similarities?

contrast between those who trust in God and those who trust in cleverness, deceit, or military strength. Probably the greatest model of faith as trust was Abraham (Genesis 15:1-6), especially since the birth of Abraham's promised heir was not conceived until a whole generation later.

As a Jewish rabbi, Jesus agreed with this basic idea that faith meant to trust God. As he spent his time with real people, he was often surprised by how little of that trust he found (Mark 6:6; 9:19; Luke 17:5-6). He was as quick to commend those who had that trust as he was to chastise those who did not.

CALMING A SEA OF DOUBT

Read Mark 4:35-41.

Mark sets this familiar story of Jesus calming the sea into a larger tale of several crossings of the Sea of Galilee that Jesus made with his disciples. The near side of the sea was Jewish territory, the far side primarily non-Jewish or Gentile land. The sea itself represented primeval chaos (Genesis 1:1-2),

and hence the wide cultural separation that existed at that time between the Jews and Gentiles. This decision of Jesus to venture to and actually do ministry on "the other side" (4:35) would have been momentously symbolic for the disciples.

It was during this crossing from the familiar to the unfamiliar, the comfortable to the threatening, that a storm arose and began to swamp the disciples' boat. In the telling of the story, the tempest can represent for us the understandable anxieties of the disciples. What business did they have, after all, bringing a Jewish rabbi to pagan lands? What would

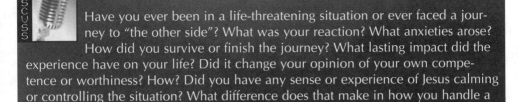

Have you ever been in a life-threatening situation or ever faced a journey to "the other side"? What was your reaction? What anxieties arose? How did you survive or finish the journey? What lasting impact did the experience have on your life? Did it change your opinion of your own competence or worthiness? How? Did you have any sense or experience of Jesus calming or controlling the situation? What difference does that make in how you handle a critical situation?

happen to them when they were rejected? Would they be thrown out, killed, or merely ignored? Throughout the Gospels, the basic competence of the disciples is up for grabs (Mark 9:17-19).

In the middle of the storm the panicked disciples woke up the peacefully slumbering Jesus and angrily accused him of not caring for their lives. He immediately and dramatically calmed the sea (thus showing that he had command over chaos, just like God in Genesis 1). Jesus' next words were pointed straight at the heart of the disciples: "Why are you afraid? Have you still no faith?" (4:40).

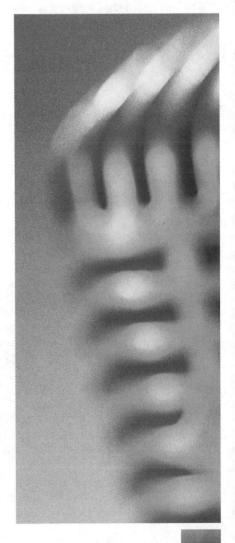

The disciples were doubly stunned, not only by this display of Jesus' power over chaos, but by the sudden exposure of their own doubts. In this story, issues of competence *and* worthiness are at stake. The disciples may have felt unsure about their ability to meet the challenge of ministering within a new culture (competence). But when the storm threatened their lives, note how the other question came to the fore: "Teacher, do you not care that we are perishing?" They were asking, in other words, "Will we end up dying meaninglessly in this storm?" Does anyone up there love us? (worthiness).

As they began to recover their wits, they stammered to one another, "Who then is this, that even the wind and the sea obey him?" The storm shocked them into realizing their vulnerability, and they began to see that the answer to their second question might be found in the identity of Jesus.

THE TWO DAUGHTERS

Interestingly, that question (who is this?) is answered in the story that follows (Mark 5:1-20). Jesus met a demoniac on the pagan side of the sea, cast out the demons, and demonstrated that he had come to heal both Jew *and* Gentile.

Read Mark 5:21-43.

After the exorcism in the Gerasenes (5:1-20), the action moves back across the sea onto Jewish territory. As a crowd gathered around Jesus again, a synagogue leader named Jairus came to Jesus to beg him to heal his daughter. A synagogue leader would have been a highly privileged and respected man. He (and those of his culture) would naturally have expected his request to gain the immediate priority of Jesus. Indeed, Jesus left the crowd and followed Jairus to his home.

Then the scene shifts abruptly and we are told of a nameless, faceless woman who reached out to take the hem of Jesus' garment and be healed. This woman was desperately poor, having spent all her money on useless medical care. For having a flow of blood, she would have been considered unclean. So for very good reason she would have assumed that Jesus would have no time for her. In fact, for him to touch her at all would have been unheard of.

But Jesus felt her presence and immediately stopped the procession. He demanded to know who had touched him, but the disciples tried to discourage the interruption. Yet the woman came to him and he blessed her, commending her faith.

BIBLE

The Two Daughters

Read Mark 5:21-43 and this section.

Which of the problems the woman faced were physical and which were social? How were they related? Who are the "unnamed women" in our society? What are some of the hurdles they face in having basic needs met? Does our culture have ways of naming certain people "unclean?" What are they?

Who are the "synagogue rulers" in our culture? What privileges do they enjoy? Do you think it was unusual for Jairus to come to Jesus for help? Why?

Both the woman and Jairus had some level of expectation or confidence in approaching Jesus. What were the differences? Where do you find hope and faith in these stories?

DISCUSS

Two Daughters Raised

Of all the characters in the story (the crowd, the woman, Jairus, the daughter, the disciples) with whom do you identify with most? Why? What difference does that identification make to you as you understand the story? Do you have any confidence that God can heal what ails you? that God can make a difference in your life? Explain.

Meanwhile, the daughter of the synagogue ruler had died. Jesus' delay over this unnamed woman must have seemed at least partly to blame.

TWO DAUGHTERS RAISED

The synagogue ruler faced a situation that despite his social privilege was utterly beyond the control of his competence. His position was of no use to him as he faced what is one of the most devastating griefs imaginable: the death of his child.

That Jesus took any time at all to attend to the woman's needs was outrageous by cultural standards. That he did so while rushing to help the privileged daughter of a synagogue ruler was incomprehensible. Yet he did. Her strength of conviction, despite twelve years of suffering and stigma, is equally remarkable.

Jesus was right to point out that it was her faith that made the difference. In the single act of reaching out to him she indicated that she refused to believe the story told about her worth in that society. She did not think of herself as unclean, unworthy, or unwanted, but that she was loved by God. Her confidence was in the right place: "Daughter, your faith has made you well; go in peace, and be healed of your disease" (5:34). His healing restored her social standing as well as her body. For the first time in her life, she became the privileged daughter.

In the end, Jesus also met Jairus's needs by raising his daughter back to life. His single command to Jairus was to let go of his privilege and be like the unnamed woman who touched Jesus' cloak. He should have faith: do not fear, only believe" (5:36). Taking the father and mother and his closest followers into the room, he told the girl to get up and then arranged for her to have a meal.

Closer Look

Imagine that you are taking a literature course and examining this story. Describe the characters that appear, using only the information contained in this text. Identify the plot twists and turns that appear as the story unfolds.

With which character or characters does the narrator (Mark) want you, the reader or listener, to identify? In what way? Is the story effective? Why? Name the point(s) or meaning(s) of the story. How effective is the story in making these points? Can you name other stories (from any sources) that are structured similarly or make similar points? Now closely compare the story as told in Matthew 9:18-26 and Luke 8:40-56. Which of these versions is most effective? Why? Does the meaning shift at all in these other retellings?

Fusing the Word With My World

Do you agree that our economy primarily awards competence? Is this the whole story of why some people earn more or are more privileged? What other elements come into play? Do you experience this time in your life as a time when you are expected to be highly competent? Name examples.

Closing

Light a candle.

Ask participants to meditate on one or more of these scenes. Resolution of the story is not as important as simply being aware of how you fill in the details.

You are a disciple and following Jesus is taking you to a new destination. It is stormy and the boat is being swamped.

You are the woman, needing to reach out in faith in a new way and trust that you are loved.

You are Jairus and are being threatened by a loss that you have no control over.

After a given amount of time (no more than ten minutes), adjourn the group session. Hold the image in your mind in the coming week. Does the story resolve itself in any particular way?

If you choose, close with the following prayer: "Eternal God, you know from where we have come and where we are going, even though we do not know these things about ourselves. Help us to have confidence based on our faith in you. Amen."

FUSING THE WORD WITH MY WORLD

We live in a culture that prizes and awards competence. In an information economy, those with the greatest social standing are those who are most highly educated and skilled. Further, as young adults we are in the prime of our competency. This is a time of our lives when we are supposed to be at our sharpest: formal education finished or nearly completed, career advancing, possessions accumulating. When our boat begins to swamp, it has become second nature to try to solve our fear by trying harder, by being more competent. We go to the mall and buy a book about it.

Yet not all of us have caught a ride on this competence-based gravy train. Maybe we have opted out on purpose and are living an intentionally simple life. Perhaps an illness, family responsibility, or lack of funds made it hard for us to get the training we wanted at this stage of our lives. Like the unnamed woman, we must look beyond the story our culture tells about us and keep our eyes fixed on the garment of divine love.

Others of us are like Jairus, learning to expect that our social privilege will solve our problems. But when the crisis hits, our lack of faith is suddenly exposed. Our deeper need to know God's love remains unmet.

Christians believe that living confidently is a gift of faith, not of privilege or competence or luck. It is not our birth into a certain social class that tells the story of our worth, but our adoption as children by God. Our knowledge of ourselves is not based on *what* we are, but *whose* we are.

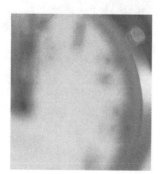

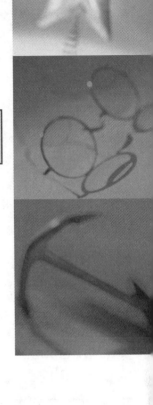

Session 3

FAITHFULNESS

> This session is designed to help participants learn
> to discern the voice of God and to know the glory
> that comes from obeying it.

BEING TRUE

Faithfulness between partners, spouses, and friends seems hard to come by in our culture. Our high divorce rate and the lurid parade of broken-down relationships on television talk shows might persuade us that cheating and backstabbing are the norm.

Is it true, as the old song says, "You always hurt the one you love"? One prophet thought so.

A PROPHET FUMES

Read Micah 7.

Micah was a Judean prophet of the eighth century B.C. from a small town south of Jerusalem. Like many small-town prophets in our own day, Micah was appalled at the sinfulness of the big city. His invective against violence, perversion, and dishonesty sounds strangely modern, as does his throw-the-hands-up-in-despair conclusion: "The faithful have disappeared from the land, / and there is no one left who is upright" (7:2).

Like someone who had been hurt badly himself, he bitterly advised his readers to

Getting Started

If you did the closing exercise from the previous session, invite group members to discuss their experience of the image they held in their minds through the week. Did it resolve itself in any interesting way? Was it forgotten?

Being True

Form small groups. Have each group try to make a list of famous and infamous examples of betrayals between persons who were close (example, Brutus killing Julius Caesar). These can be examples from fiction, history, or current events. After five minutes compare your lists with one another.

Do you think it is true that faithfulness is more rare today than it has been in the past? Or does faithfulness look different today? What forms of faithfulness/ unfaithfulness are particularly relevant to persons who are in their twenties and thirties?

A Prophet Fumes

BIBLE

Read Micah 6:9–7:8 to get the whole series of Micah's indictments against the city and its inhabitants. The prophet connects the people's unfaithfulness to God as the cause of their unfaithfulness to one another. To what extent do you think it is true that people's ability to love others grows out of their religious lives? What exceptions can you name? Do you think that the problems of our cities would be significantly improved if more people were religious? loved God? Why or why not?

Put no trust in a friend,
  have no confidence in a loved one;
guard the doors of your mouth
  from her who lies in your embrace; . . .

your enemies are members of
  your own household (7:5-6).

BEING FAITHFUL

We may not have drunk the cup of bitterness as deeply as Micah, but by this stage in our lives we have probably been hurt more than once by those we love. We have probably also hurt others with our own unfaithfulness. All of our close relationships are characterized by this fundamental risk that they will someday fall apart through betrayal or mistrust. Sometimes the risk of being hurt makes our hearts so hard that like Micah we push others away. But astoundingly, more often we pick ourselves up and enter the risk of relationship all over again.

Now come the hard questions: What do we do when God seems to be unfaithful to us? What is the difference between having faith in God and being faithful ourselves to God? What happens when our relationship with God breaks down?

THE RELUCTANT PROPHET

Moby Dick, Pinocchio, and Jaws—a monster fish comes out of the murky depths and swallows up someone. For many of us, that's about all we can recall about Jonah too. But the story of Jonah is much more interesting and complex than the fish tale alone. For the remainder of this session, we will take some time to mine this story for what it has to say about our faithfulness to God, and God's faithfulness to us.

Read Jonah 1.

The Book of Jonah is included in the section of the Old Testament recording the sayings of twelve "minor prophets." But it is really a short story rather than a collection of sermons. It was probably written between 500 and 400 B.C., during or after the capture and deportation of the Jews to Assyria. It is a morality tale whose main character is a prophet who apparently lived some two hundred years before the story was written (2 Kings 14:25).

Perhaps the writer of the story chose the obscure prophet Jonah to be the main character of the story because his name meant "dove." The dove would have been immediately recognized by readers as a traditional symbol for Israel (Psalm 74:19; Hosea 11:11).

In the story's opening, Jonah is called as Micah was by Yahweh to preach against the wickedness of the city. Nineveh, the "great city," was the capital of Assyria, the very nation that had defeated and enslaved Israel. Jonah's (Israel's) call to preach repentance to them was no doubt sickening. Surely, Yahweh should be destroying, not saving, the hated enemy of Israel.

So instead of obeying Yahweh, Jonah flees to Tarshish, a city as far away from Nineveh in the east as one could go in those

Being Faithful

Can you recall a time when you experienced or practiced unfaithfulness? What was behind it? What was particularly shocking or hurtful about this? What was the long-term result on the relationship? On other relationships that followed?

Have you ever experienced a time when God seemed unfaithful to you? What was that like? What did you do? What, do you think, is the difference between having faith in God and being faithful to God?

The Reluctant Prophet

Before you begin reading Jonah, ask what participants can recall about the story. Write these down on a piece of paper to compare with what you discover as the session moves forward. At the end of the session, discuss how accurate your memory of the story seemed to be. What was forgotten? How important were the things you remembered relative to what you now think is important in the story? Where did these memories come from? Do you suspect the rest of your recall of the Bible is of about the same reliability as your recall of Jonah? Why or why not?

Teaching Hint: Read the story of Jonah aloud, having group members take turns. Encourage the group to experience it like the comical short story that it is, rather than as a historical record.

days. Jonah's attempt to get away from Yahweh takes him to the very bottom of a ship, where he waits out a storm that Yahweh sends. But a throw of the dice exposes Jonah as the cause of the storm. Note the contrast between the faith that Jonah professes as a Hebrew (1:9) and the growing faithfulness to Yahweh that the pagan sailors demonstrate (1:14-16).

Jonah's head doesn't seem screwed on right at this point. He describes God as the one who "made the sea and the dry land" (1:9) but tries to escape this God by getting on a boat. In fact, Jonah is so adamant about not doing what Yahweh requests that he chooses to die (1:12; see also 4:3, 8). But Jonah's plan gets foiled when Yahweh sends a fish (not a whale) to swallow him.

THE FISH PRAYER

Read Jonah 2.

Not surprisingly, the experience of being in the fish's belly changes Jonah and he begins to pray. At first we expect he will pray for help, but it turns out that this is a prayer of thanksgiving for deliverance. The incongruity here between Jonah's praise of

The Reluctant Prophet
This story begins with the normal Old Testament prophetic pattern: "The word of the Lord came to Jonah."

■ How do we know what God is saying to us or wants us to do?

■ Are there methods you use to discern God's will for your life? What are they?

Jonah demonstrates that it is quite possible for people to know the right thing to do and do exactly the opposite.

■ Have you ever, like Jonah, sought to flee from something God wanted? What happened?

■ Do you think it is OK to argue with God? If so, to what extent?

■ What are some of the things that make God's call on your life difficult?

Faith: Living a Spiritual Life

God and his earlier flight from God suggests to some scholars that the prayer was a later insertion into the story by an editor.

Others argue that Jonah's yearning to return to the Temple (2:4, 7) is a veiled expression of Israel's hope to escape from the Assyrian exile. As it stands in the story now, Jonah's song of faith seems to result in Yahweh's change of mind; God orders the fish to save Jonah.

Other commentators have wondered whether the writer intended us to think that the song, with its saccharine piety and overly fond remembrance of the Temple, caused the fish literally to vomit ("spew") him up onto land. In any case, after being deposited unceremoniously on the beach, Jonah soon began to obey Yahweh, if only resentfully.

The Fish Prayer

Read the prayer or song of Jonah in 2:2-10. What are the elements of this prayer? What does it say about God? to God? Does this prayer strike you as being sincere or ironic for Jonah? Is the reader intended to believe that Jonah is genuine in his piety and repentance or trying to manipulate God? What leads you to believe this?

THE BIG CITY REPENTS

Read Jonah 3.

Jonah's sermon in the big city (3:4) is not a portrait of rhetorical brilliance. It contains exactly five words in Hebrew. This and several other matters in this chapter suggest that we are dealing here with mythic story-telling rather than historical record:

- First, Nineveh has been excavated by archaeologists who have found that it was never more than three miles long or a mile and a half wide, clearly not the three-day and three-night journey depicted in 3:3 (which is clearly a literary echo of the time he spent in the fish; see 1:17).
- Second, the almost comic spasms of the city to fast and to put sackcloth on themselves and their animals after a five-word sermon far exceeds any kind of faithfulness ever expressed by Israel itself.
- Third, being the capital city of Assyria,

Closer Look

Jonah prays for deliverance from "Sheol" (2:2). Sheol was the place of the dead in Hebrew myth. Do some research on the meaning and function of Sheol in the Old Testament.

The Big City Repents

Read Jonah 3. What purpose does it serve to have the city portrayed as so large in this story? the sermon so short? the spasmodic repentance?

The story relates that God's mind was changed about destroying the Ninevites after seeing their repentance. Can God's mind really be changed like this? Or is this simply an element in the story that is useful for the plot? Do you think that God can have a change of heart about some things and not others? Could God decide to destroy the universe on a whim? Could God choose not to be just or merciful? What things do you think God could or would not choose to do? Why?

SMALL GROUP

The Punchline

Break into small groups to talk about Israel's unwillingness to think of the Assyrians as people for whom God cared. How does religion serve to isolate groups of people from those who are different from them? From what groups, if any, does your church's practice of faith effectively isolate you? For example, a church in the suburbs may be isolated from poverty, or a church that is not handicapped accessible may isolate itself from those who need ramps. What would it mean to be faithful to these people? Is such isolation always bad or wrong? Explain.

had Nineveh actually come to believe in Yahweh, the subsequent history of Israel and the Middle East would have been completely different from what we know actually happened.

But the story's hyperbole of Nineveh's faithfulness serves admirably as a contrast to Jonah's (Israel's) own miserly faith. Is the writer trying to make a point about the prayers for deliverance expressed by Israel during its exile (as Jonah did in the fish in Chapter 2)? Were there ways of being faithful in the midst of exile that were more important and more in keeping with God's character than wishing things would just go back to the way they used to be?

THE PUNCHLINE

Read Jonah 4.

Now we get to the heart of Jonah's reason for fleeing to Tarshish in the first place: he knows down deep that Yahweh is gracious and merciful. Even now, Jonah would rather die than live with the knowledge that he was the instrument through which God saved the Assyrians (4:3). Like the nation of Israel that he represents, Jonah cannot shake the conviction that as a Jew he is more specially loved by God than non-Jews are. As George Orwell said about the pigs in *Animal Farm*, they are "more equal" than others.

Still hopeful that mayhem would rain down from heaven on the city, Jonah sulks under a booth or tent. He must have thought that the miraculous growth of the shady bush or bean plant over him signaled that God had returned to a "right" frame of mind and was caring for him especially. But the death of the plant and the hot wind and the sun show Jonah that the "Hound of Heaven" is not quite done with him yet.

God then puts Jonah on the spot with a simple question that uncovers his error: Why do you care more about the death of this plant than the fate of an entire city of my people? God's true nature is then made plain, as is the reason why God asked Jonah to be faithful in this particular way. Despite what they may have done in capturing and enslaving Israel, God deeply cares for the people, and yes, even the animals of Assyria. In other words, Jonah's call to preach was God's way of showing this love. How dare Jonah run away from it!

DIVINE FAITHFULNESS

We began our session with some reflections on what it means to be faithful in a loving relationship. We have just finished a story that clearly states a fundamental truth held by the biblical witness: that in the loving relationship between God and human beings, God is always the faithful one, not us.

Jonah had faith, but he was not very faithful. He was a true believer and a near miraculous preacher. At times his understanding of God was painfully confused and selfish, but there were other moments of absolute clarity. He worshiped a Creator (1:9) who is utterly merciful and gracious (4:2).

In the midst of their enslavement by the Assyrians, Israel was asking hard questions about God's faithfulness. God's answer in this story, as unsatisfying as it might have been to them, was that there were ways of being faithful that they were overlooking. God's call to them was not to return to some idyllic temple worship, but to engage their captors in the faith they held so dear.

Closing
Read Psalm 36:5-9 aloud or in unison.

Then pray together the following prayer:

"O God, as you call me to service through your word, your messengers, and the needs that I see in the world, give me the love, strength, courage, and wisdom to discern and to respond so that I, even I, may dare to make a difference in this world. Amen."

FUSING THE WORD WITH MY WORLD

The faithfulness of God apparently extends to persons far beyond ourselves, to people who hate and misuse us, to those who are not at all religious in the "right way," and even to the whole of the created order: cattle, bushes, worms, and big fish. The God who loves us and whom we love is "unfaithful" to us in that sometimes frustrating respect: God loves everyone else too. When our faith in God becomes cloying and narrow, we have misjudged the character of the one we claim to love. God makes love with the whole world, not just us. And this matters deeply in how we choose to live.

FAITH THAT SAVES

This session is designed to explore the relationship between faith and salvation, comparing the insights of Jesus and Paul.

AN OVERUSED WORD

Let's begin by recognizing that "salvation" and "being saved" are strange religious terms that mean different things to different people. They are also terms that tend to provoke strong opinions and disagreements among Christians. It might help loosen our conversation to begin thinking of the ways we use the word *save* in non-religious ways.

- We *save* money by using coupons.
- A soccer goalie makes a great *save*.
- We *save* aluminum cans for recycling.
- A lifeguard *saves* a drowning swimmer.
- Money we don't intend to spend right away goes into a *savings* account.
- Community activists try to *save* old buildings from demolition.
- We *save* our computer files.
- We are discussing all the meanings of salvation *save* religious ones.

In these non-religious examples, generally people are the ones trying to save something or someone. Religious uses of the words *saved* or *salvation* usually imply that it is not us but God who is doing the saving and that people themselves are the ones who are "saved."

Getting Started

Check in with one another.

Write a quick response (as you can) to the following three questions.

- *From* what do human beings need to be saved?
- *For* what do we need to be saved?
- What is the difference between someone who is saved and someone who is not?

Check responses without any additional explanations. Are the answers mostly similar or different? Is this a difficult subject for you to talk about? Explain.

An Overused Word

List as many examples as you can think of for ways to use *save* in everyday, non-religious conversation. Add to this a list of non-religious ways that we use *salvation*. Are there a certain number of core definitions you can identify? Do you ever use the words *salvation* or *being saved* in an explicitly religious way? How often? In what contexts? What do you mean by it?

TWO LEVELS

Two Levels

Read John 3:16-17. This is one of the most famous passages in the Bible. Note how this passage includes both levels of salvation: What God does and what effect that has on the world.

Christians use the term *salvation* in two basic ways. The first meaning refers to what God has done and is doing to bring the world back into a proper or loving relationship with God. Christians particularly think of salvation as the "saving work" of God in Jesus Christ.

At a second level, Christians talk about salvation as an experience or event that happens to people. Some of the many different ways Christians have understood the human dimension of salvation include being:

- made a whole person;
- healed of disease;
- liberated from political oppression or slavery;
- forgiven for our sins;
- freed of the tendency to sin;
- guaranteed a place in heaven;
- made a member of Christ's church through baptism;
- restored to right relationship with God;
- restored to right relationship with the earth and other living beings;
- made perfect in love.

Each of these meanings can be found in the Bible. Each has been stressed at one time or another by theologians or Christian groups depending on the time and culture in which they lived or the tradition or social class to which they belonged.

SALVATION IN JESUS' MINISTRY

The ministry of Jesus was remarkable in that he extended the offer of salvation to those who were sinners (Mark 2:16-17). He caused a scandal among the religious leaders of his day for paying attention to those who were considered unclean and unfit for salvation: tax collectors, prostitutes, the poor, and the sick (Matthew 21:31; Luke 14:16-24). He told a striking parable of two men, one a righteous Pharisee and one a tax collector. While the religious man gloated over how good he was, the tax man confessed his sin and was thereby accepted by God (Luke 18:9-14).

For Jesus, salvation could mean physical healing, the forgiveness of sins, or both (Mark 2:1-12). The Greek word *sozo* used in the Gospels means "to save" and also "to heal or make whole." Usually faith was a precondition for salvation (Mark 5:34; 10:52; Luke 17:19; but note that sometimes Jesus healed people whether they had faith or not. See, for example, Mark 3:1-5). In one story (Luke 7:36-50), an unnamed woman demonstrated her repentance by anointing Jesus' feet with oil and then wiping them with her hair. In the face of sharp criticism for allowing this behavior, Jesus told the woman that her sins were forgiven, stating explicitly that "Your faith has saved you; go in peace" (7:50). In the story of Zacchaeus, a wealthy tax collector (Luke 19:1-10), Jesus pronounced that salvation had come to him after Zacchaeus gave away half of his possessions to the poor and promised to repay those he cheated.

As one reads the stories of Jesus healing persons and pronouncing forgiveness, it becomes clear that for those who met Jesus,

SMALL GROUP

Two Levels

In small groups, read this list and discuss which of these images is closest to what you understand by the human experience of salvation and to your church or tradition. See if you can add to this list other ways Christians or non-Christians sometimes talk about the experience of salvation. Discuss whether you think salvation is something that happens to you at one moment in time or is a longer process. If a process, does it ever end or come to a conclusion? Why or why not?

BIBLE

Salvation in Jesus' Ministry

Read and study one of these stories more carefully, or divide them among three smaller groups, then compare findings together.

- Luke 18:9-14
- Mark 2:1-12
- Luke 7:36-50

In each story, think about the characters involved. What seem to be their motivations for what they do or say? What evidence of faith do they demonstrate? Is this always something verbal? What is the result of Jesus' interaction with them? What does salvation look like for them?

Wholeness and Salvation

What does it mean to "be made whole?" What would the life of a person who was whole look like? Make a list of these characteristics. Do you or have you known anyone who exemplifies what salvation can do for people? Name them and explain your reasons.

Then talk about the idea that salvation looks different for different people according to their needs or lives. Play with this idea as a group by agreeing on a television drama, movie, or book that everyone in your group knows. List the characters in the story and the key shortcomings or problems they have. What would salvation look like in each case?

salvation (wholeness or healing) came to them in different ways. Those who were sinners were forgiven, those who were sick were healed, and those who were rich gave to the poor. Faith in God led to an experience of salvation that struck each person at the heart of his or her life and self-understanding.

SALVATION BY FAITH IN PAUL'S LETTERS

Many Christians have taken what Paul said about faith and salvation as the centerpiece of their understanding and experience of Christianity rather than the Gospel accounts of Jesus. In fact, the Christian church has often experienced renewed energy and certainty of purpose when it has "rediscovered" Paul's classic doctrine of "justification by faith."

Read Romans 1:16-17; 3:21-26.

For Paul faith was something very specific: belief in Jesus Christ. But this faith was not just a matter of knowing about Jesus and believing he was the example for us to follow. Nor was it the effort we make to practice what he preached or to be like him in our love of God and others. Faith for Paul was rather a personal trust in the work that God accomplished through the suffering, death, and resurrection of Jesus.

Biblical Studies 101: Paul and Jesus

Paul never met Jesus, and apparently either did not know much about his life or never thought it was important enough to write much about. An exception that proves the rule is found in 1 Corinthians 11:23-26, where Paul describes what Jesus did at the Last Supper. This table ritual was one of the most distinctive and important marks of the early Christians. It is not surprising, therefore, that Paul would have to deal with its practice in his letters to the early churches.

Paul's understanding of "what was accomplished" included a number of important assumptions.

First, Paul thought that the whole of humanity is under the curse of sin. He understood this historically through the story of Adam and Eve who chose to disobey God and then passed on both the tendency to disobey and the consequence of disobedience: death (Romans 5:12-14).

Second, Paul held that it was impossible for human beings to recover their relationship to God by their own efforts. The grand attempt at this had been to try to follow the commandments of the Old Testament, the law. While the law helped clarify what God demanded of human behavior, it did not empower human beings to live that way. So, Paul taught, whether you were Jewish and tried to follow the law, or non-Jewish (Greek) and knew nothing of the law, practically speaking, you were in the same boat (Romans 3:9).

Third, while it was impossible for human beings to either restore their relationship with God or to overcome death by trying hard to live correctly, it was not impossible for God to do. God chose to do this through Jesus Christ. It was sheer love for humanity (grace) that caused God to allow the death of Jesus on the cross also to be the death of sin (Romans 3:23-25).

Fourth, the gospel or good news of Jesus Christ for Paul was the announcement that everyone, both Jew and Greek, can participate in the victory of Jesus over sin and death through faith (1:16-17). It becomes effective when we put our faith in this promise rather than in our own efforts to save ourselves. We have to believe in it (Galatians 3:5).

Salvation by Faith in Paul's Letters

Read Romans 1:16-17; 3:21-26, then look at the four assumptions that lie behind Paul's understanding of salvation by faith. Which of these assumptions do you share and which do you reject? Specifically:

- Do you think that human death is a result of sin or part of what it means to be a species on this planet? Are there ways that human beings encounter death because of evil and sin that they wouldn't otherwise? (Romans 5:12-14).
- Is it really impossible for human beings to reconnect with God through their own efforts? How far can we get? (Romans 3:9).
- How do you think the execution of Jesus on the cross effected the reconciliation of God and humanity? What questions or objections to this idea can be named? (Romans 3:23-25).
- How do you think the execution of Jesus on the cross effected the reconciliation of God and humanity? What questions or objections to this idea can be named? (Romans 3:23-25).
- What potential misunderstandings can arise if we believe that only faith can save us? What problems does it solve? (Romans 1:16-17; Galatians 3:5; Ephesians 2:8-9).

Faith That Saves

A Changed Life
Read Romans 6:1-14. Get together in small groups and talk about your own baptism and/or your understanding of baptism. Given the meaning that Paul attaches to baptism, would you defend or argue against the practice of infant baptism? Why? Do you think the amount of water used changes its meaning in any way? Why or why not?

Paul says, "No longer present your members to sin as instruments of wickedness, but as instruments of righteousness" (6:13). In practical terms, what would this mean for you? What is your understanding of sin? If sin dies in Christians who are "born again" or baptized, why do they have to continue to struggle against it in themselves?

Is salvation something that occurs at baptism and the moment that one accepts Christ by faith? Or is it something that happens when sin has finally and completely died in a person? Do you think being sinless includes being free of making mistakes?

A classic statement from the Letter to the Ephesians underlines the important idea that salvation is a matter of God's love: "For by grace you have been saved through faith, and this is not your own doing; it is the gift of God—not the result of works, so that no one may boast" (2:8-9).

A CHANGED LIFE

Read Romans 6:1-14.

Paul was a rabbi and had once been a persecutor of Christians until Christ appeared to him in a vision while traveling on the road to Damascus (Galatians 1:13-17; Acts 9:1-22). That he became the foremost missionary of Christ to the Greek-speaking world shows the radical change his encounter with Jesus engendered.

Paul understood the experience of accepting the gift of God's grace in Jesus Christ as a death and a rebirth. The sign of that death and rebirth was baptism. In going under the water Christians ritually enact their own death and burial with Jesus. In coming up out of the water, they enact Christ's resurrection and new life. What "dies" at baptism is death and sin, and what lives is a new creature free to live by God's grace.

Of course, even Christians who have this experience of being "born again" still struggle to live within their new reality. Paul acknowledges this powerfully in Romans 7:19: "For I do not do the good I want, but the evil I do not want is what I do."

REFLECTIONS ON THE WORD

We have explored two different understandings of faith and salvation in this session, that of the Gospel accounts of Jesus and that of Paul. Comparing the two leaves us some issues to consider:

- For Jesus salvation was a matter of healing and wholeness, while for Paul it had to do with victory over the power of sin and death.
- For Jesus salvation tended to look different for different people according to their situation and need, while for Paul everyone was in the same boat (Jew and Greek), and the pattern of salvation similar for all persons.
- For Paul there is an exclusive emphasis on the death and resurrection of Jesus as the cause of our salvation. The Gospels indicate that Jesus brought salvation to human beings through his life, teaching, and healing ministries; of course, they also end with the story of the Crucifixion and the Resurrection.

Both Jesus and Paul connected salvation with faith and the sheer love of God rather than one's achievements or moral attainments. Christianity was agreed on this fundamental point: that God's love is given to all as a gift. The appropriate response to that gift is faith.

DISCUSS

Reflections on the Word

Look at these comparisons of Paul and Jesus on salvation by faith. Which of them do you find closer to your own views? Which of them is closer to what you hear in your church? What strengths and weaknesses are present in each view? How would you describe your own experience of salvation?

DISCUSS

Fusing the Word With My World

What is the difference between faith-in-general and the heart of the Christian faith as described here? Is Christian faith something you have or want for yourself? Why or why not? If you have not been previously baptized, is this something that you might want for yourself? What steps can you take to find out more about these things?

FUSING THE WORD WITH MY WORLD

Closing

As a closing prayer, have someone read aloud Psalm 51:1-12 while others listen with their eyes closed.

We can save money, time, stamps, shots on goals, computer files, and drowning swimmers, but to hear the witness of Jesus and Paul, we cannot save ourselves. Only God can and does.

The faith that Christians claim is not a faith-in-general, a starry-eyed hope that people are good and that things will work out in the end. Christian faith is very specific: what God does through the life and death of Christ remakes us in God's image. To combine insights from our studies of Jesus and Paul, maybe when it comes to salvation we are all alike and all different at the same time: we all need salvation, but what that will look like for each of us will radically depend on who we are.

Salvation is a rope that God the lifeguard throws to those of us who are under the waves and sinking fast. Faith is the hand that grabs it.

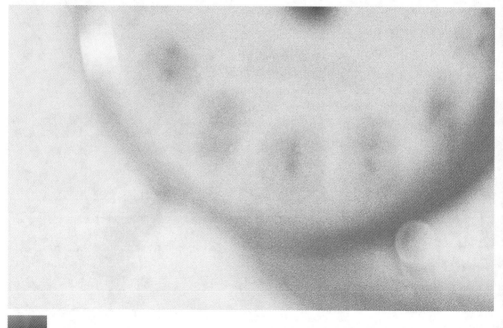

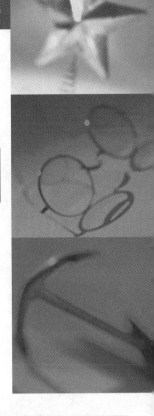

FAITH AND ACTION

This session will explore what responsibilities come with the profession of faith in Jesus Christ.

DOING GOOD, DOING EVIL

Talking about faith and studying the Bible are important steps for learning the Christian life. However, the real test comes when you step out on faith and dare to make a difference in the world. There is a correlation between true faith and the acceptance of social responsibility.

It is common knowledge that Christians are supposed to put their faith to action. Many Christians do this in remarkable and sacrificial ways by:

- working at the food pantry;
- building homes for the homeless;
- bringing relief to disaster victims;
- providing shelter for abused women and their children;
- standing vigil outside a state prison during an execution;
- raising money for minority scholarships;
- living simply and giving the remainder for refugee ministries;
- working as a lobbyist for environmental causes.

But unfortunately that is not the whole story. No one who knows history is unaware of the ugly past of Christianity:

Getting Started

Draw a line down a chalkboard or piece of paper. Brainstorm for one minute and list in the left column as many contemporary problems as you can name (pass out newspapers or newsmagazines if desired). Brainstorm for another minute to list in the right column things individuals can do to help solve each problem.

For which problems was it easiest to imagine personal responses? Which were most difficult? Why? Circle those problems for which you think you cannot be a part of a solution.

- converting people at swordpoint;
- sending crusaders against Muslims;
- burning dissenters at the stake;
- promoting anti-Semitism and racism;
- being slow to promote social policies that benefit the poor;
- excluding strangers and isolating themselves from the poor;
- resisting women's equality.

In these and many other ways Christians have denied Jesus and broken God's heart. No one should ignore or minimize these horrors in any way.

All Christians live within the paradox of knowing the high call of the gospel of Jesus yet never living up to it. It is a waste of breath to call the church hypocritical. Christians know this all too well already. They may have experienced salvation, but very few indeed are completely and utterly saved.

In the remainder of this session, we will examine a passage of one of the early social prophets who tried to hold Christians accountable to their faith.

THE LETTER OF JAMES

The Letter of James was controversial from its appearance. James (probably not James the brother of Jesus) wrote this letter—really a book of wisdom and moral instruction—to Jewish converts to Christianity. He was concerned that the Pauline emphasis on salvation by faith alone had led some Christians into a lackadaisical attitude about how they actually lived their lives: if God saved them by grace, not by works, they concluded, then what they did simply didn't matter much (although this conclusion was certainly not shared by Paul himself). But for James, true faith should manifest itself in good works, otherwise it can hardly be called faith at all.

But James's call back to righteous living was worrisome to adherents to the Pauline understanding of faith, who thought it would confuse Christians into thinking they could be saved by their own actions. Few of the early theologians of the church mentioned or quoted from the letter. And Martin Luther, who began the Protestant Reformation with a renewed emphasis on Paul's doctrine of salvation by faith, called it "an epistle of straw." But the book was included in the Latin Bible at the end of the fourth century and stayed in our New Testaments despite periodic attempts to banish it. The majority of Christians have recognized that its strong moral and social expectations for people who dare to call themselves Christian provides a needed counterpoint to Paul's rather personal and spiritualistic understanding of faith.

PLACES OF PRIVILEGE

Chapter 2 of the letter was the heart of the controversy, and where James most clearly confronts the "salvation by faith alone" school of thinking.

Read James 2:1-13.

This chapter begins with a sarcastic question (2:1): Is it possible that given the way you treat the poor you are really followers of Jesus? It isn't precisely clear what was happening in the Christian gatherings that earned James's scorn here, but in some way it involved preferential treatment in seating for the wealthy and the exclusion or

Closer Look

Does it surprise you that there was so much controversy about including the Letter of James in the New Testament? Find a good study Bible or Bible dictionary and read more about how the New Testament developed into the form we have today.

SMALL GROUP

Places of Privilege

Come up with a more thorough description of what you think was happening in the churches James condemns. Use your imagination. As a group come up with a list of contemporary Christian practices that make distinctions between rich and poor. How are the rich privileged or held up for honor in churches? How are the poor excluded or denied among some churches? Be specific. What signs of honor or exclusion can you identify in your own congregation or one in which you have been a part?

Read Leviticus 19:11-18 and compare it to James 2:1-13. Also compare the passage to Jesus' answer to the question about the most important commandments in Mark 12:28-34; Matthew 22:34-40; and Luke 10:25-28. What commandment did Jesus place before the love of neighbor? In what ways is this addition important or unimportant?

disregard of the poor. These Christians had forgotten that Jesus himself was poor and that his ministry had been chiefly among the poor. Their fawning deference to the wealthy had clouded their judgment, and thereby imperiled their faith.

Nor, James continues in 2:8-13, was it any use for them to claim that their attention to the other matters of the law excused this behavior. Living faithfully, he argues, is not like visiting a salad bar from which we can pick and choose what we like and leave behind what is not to our taste. God requires one's whole life to reflect the character of God. Here James particularly mentions the attribute of *mercy*. Any form of religion that neglects to extend to others what God has extended to us is completely bankrupt.

James drew from Leviticus 19:11-18 to prove his argument. God's law given to Moses explicitly forbade preferential or biased judgements: "You shall not render an unjust judgment; you shall not be partial to the poor or defer to the great: with justice you shall judge your neighbor" (19:15). This section of Leviticus, in fact, concludes with the famous saying, "You shall love your neighbor as yourself" (19:18). Just as Jesus did (Mark 12:28-34), James tried to refocus the spiritual life of his hearers on what was most important of all: the concrete practice of love.

Closer Look

Read Matthew 18:23-35, a powerful parable about a man who did not exercise the same kind of mercy that he had been granted. Look up the passage in a Bible commentary to better understand the values of the debt and the implications of the exaggerations Jesus employed in this parable.

Faith: Living a Spiritual Life

MERE WORDS

Read James 2:14-26.

James doesn't hold back any punches. He pointedly asks his audience whether they think their faith will save them (2:14). Then he uncovers the true nature of religious hypocrisy: It is exceedingly cruel because it wraps evil in a mantle of God-talk. Those who claim to follow Jesus supposedly make substantial promises to God and neighbor. Not to live up to those promises is like taking the bread out of the mouths of the hungry, or taking clothes away from those who have nothing. Faith by itself, as some self-involved private spirituality, is not faith at all; it is a form of death.

In 2:18-19, James holds out the same distinction we made in the first session, that faith and belief are two different things. Belief alone is no accomplishment and earns no favor from God; after all, "even the demons believe and shudder" (2:19).

He then very cleverly reverses an argument that Paul had made. In Romans 4:3-25, Paul argued that the story of Abraham showed that God accepted Abraham based on his faith, not his works. James uses the same story about Abraham (Genesis 15:1-6) to make the entirely opposite point. God promised Abraham offspring, and Abraham's belief of God at that time was certainly righteous. But that belief was put to the test and proven only when Abraham was asked to sacrifice his son Isaac. James's point is that Abraham's faith didn't mean much until it was actually tested. He goes so far as to directly contradict Paul when he writes, "You see that a person is justified by works and not by faith alone" (James 2:24).

Mere Words

As a group discuss this statement that privatized faith is a kind of death. In what ways does a strictly personal religion "kill"? Do you agree or disagree with this metaphor? Why? Review James 2:14-26 to help refine your thinking.

Closer Look

Read Genesis 15:1-6 and 22:1-14. Then read Paul's discussion of Abraham in Romans 4:3-25 and compare it with James's argument. With which of these writers do you agree most? Did Abraham's faith come at the point of belief or the point of testing? Why? What is your take on this story of God calling Abraham to sacrifice his son Isaac? Is this a representation of a cruel and primitive God or a metaphor for the meaning of faith as giving everything to God? Should this story be taught to children? Why or why not?

Beyond Cheap Grace
In what way is this part of your life a "transition" to something else? In what ways are you making decisions that will affect your future? Have you had to let go of any important dreams or desires to pursue other ones? In what ways have the decisions you have made about work, family, and education affected your religious life? helped it? hindered it?

BEYOND CHEAP GRACE

Most of us desire success and stability in our lives. This is a period in which we are working hard to accumulate the education and experience we need. We are beginning to move into the second and third phases of our careers or working lives. We are forming families and settling down.

We are also making choices about lifestyle, values, and vocation that will sketch out the path of our future. Naturally, we all want to fulfill the promises that are hidden in the talents given to us by God. In doing all this, of course, we hope not to get caught up in the whirlwinds of acquisition and promotion. We pray that our journey of faith will keep us centered on what is truly important:

- reaching out to others regardless of wealth or social standing;
- recognizing that our talents belong to the community, not simply to ourselves;
- making job choices that add value and meaning to the world;
- providing a safe and nurturing home life for our families;
- being kind to strangers;
- passing our traditions down to our children.

SMALL GROUP
Break into small groups and draw up your own list of "what is truly important." Name your ultimate values. Now relate to one another in what ways you live out these values in your present life. Name some ways that you aspire to live them out more fully. What role does your faith play in these ultimate values?

But James throws a bucket of cold water on any idea that faith can be "just one more part" of our busy lives. In the end, faith will claim us entirely or it will wither and die. We cannot, as James pointed out in his own day, play the game of preferentialism now and still call ourselves followers of Jesus.

That we cannot have it both ways, of course, is not a popular idea, particularly in the church. We can very much appreciate why early Christians (and Christians ever since!) were attracted to a gospel that gave them the benefit of feeling they were loved and accepted by God without having to experience any risk or cost to themselves. The German theologian and church leader Dietrich Bonhoeffer called this "cheap grace." His own powerful and complicated journey of faith led him to conspire to kill Hitler and eventually to be executed in a Nazi prison shortly before it was liberated by the Allies.

As Bonhoeffer found out, the directions God's grace may take us are wildly unpredictable. It will be both adventurous and costly. But the farther we penetrate into the heart of Christ the more it sinks in that the grace we have (quite undeservedly) received begs to be given away to others.

Think about the risks and costs of Christianity. Is there any way in which faith has cost you, or may cost you in the future? What risks has your faith driven you to? In what unexpected directions has your faith taken you?

Discuss the example of Dietrich Bonhoeffer. Do you believe that obeying God could ever involve murder or other very extreme behavior? Why or why not? Should Christians be in the armed forces? Why or why not?

FUSING THE WORD WITH MY WORLD

What will the faith we profess actually look like in our lives? Will we dedicate our lives to help the homeless? Choose a lesser job that gives us free time with our families? Buy a smaller car that saves money and pollutes less? Volunteer at the blood center? Work in the public defender's office? Care for our ailing parents in our own home? Adopt an "unwanted" child?

There are obviously many ways our talents and inclinations can take us. Our individual path of faith will go its own way. Praying for discernment is a crucial part of the life of faith.

To our everlasting chagrin, Jesus taught his disciples that "whoever wishes to become great among you must be your servant, and whoever wishes to be first among

Fusing the Word With My World

What does it mean to "pray for discernment"? How do you know what God wants you to do or not to do? What role does servanthood play in how your faith is acted out? Is there any decision you are facing in your life now that you would like to have discernment about? Briefly name this to the group and ask one another for prayer.

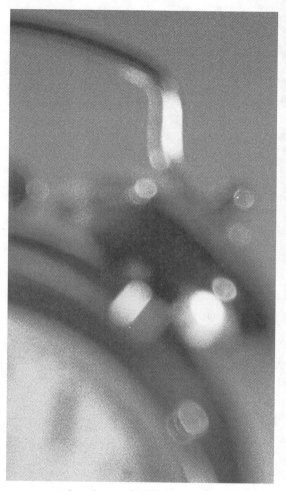

Closing

Let someone in the group read one or both of the following verses aloud. Pause between readings. Meditate on them in silence.

"I can do all things through him who strengthens me" (Philippians 4:13).

"I am the vine, you are the branches. Those who abide in me and I in them bear much fruit, because apart from me you can do nothing" (John 15:5).

If desired, pray the following to close your time of meditation: "Redeemer God, as your purpose for my life becomes clear, grant me courage and strength to carry out your will. Let my life be a testimony to my faith in you. I will always be mindful to give you the praise and glory. Amen."

you must be slave of all" (Mark 10:43-44). Being a servant or a slave for the sake of others is probably not what we had imagined for our lives. No wonder so few desire to do it.

James insisted that those who dare call themselves believers in "our glorious Lord Jesus Christ" (James 2:1) envision a world of justice, for poor and rich alike. Robert Kennedy often used this quote from Bertrand Russell: "Some people see things as they are and ask why; others see things that have never been and ask why not?" When we put faith to action we ask "why not?" And then offer ourselves as the answer.

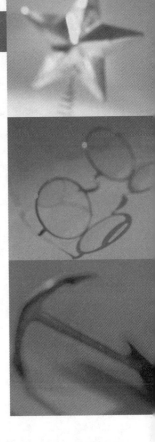

FAITH AS KNOWLEDGE OF JESUS

This session explores themes in the Gospel of John. We will consider more deeply how our faith is connected to what we believe.

FAITH AND BELIEF REVISITED

In Session 1 we pointed out that Jesus made a pretty strong distinction between faith and belief. It is important to understand that being a follower of Jesus is more a matter of what you invest your life in than what ideas you have in your head. But what you invest in and what you believe are very closely related. Just ask,

- an environmental activist who fights to save endangered species because she believes all animals have a right to thrive on this finite planet.
- a father who refuses to beat his children as his own father had done because he believes there are better ways to discipline one's children.
- a young couple who seeks out pastoral counseling for marital problems because they believe the vows they made to one another on their wedding day were important.

What you have faith in and what you believe in your head are intimately related. As many contemporary religious seekers

Getting Started

Check in with each other. If appropriate, ask if any of the questions that were raised for spiritual discernment at the end of the last session are any clearer now.

This session examines the Gospel of John, which tries to lead readers to some very specific conclusions about the identity of Jesus. As you begin, discuss your own current ideas about the identity of Jesus. Briefly go around the room and say a couple of sentences about who you think Jesus was and how you came to think this way.

have discovered, you can't really have faith in things you don't believe to be real or true. For those seekers, many of the answers that traditional religions give do not fit the questions the world is asking today. They want a faith that helps them to live in the postmodern world. These seekers know that at some point your faith has to engage your brain or it will become meaningless (at best) or harmful (at worst).

THIS IS YOUR BRAIN

In their book, *The Humanizing Brain*, James B. Ashbrook and Carol Rausch Albright (Cleveland: The Pilgrim Press, 1997) point out that when we are born, our brains consist of billions of nerve cells, or neurons, but they are mostly unconnected to one another. Some connections are made naturally as we grow, like those that help us to walk. But many other pathways develop uniquely, reflecting the culture, family, habits, and beliefs we learn. As our experiences change, we actually grow new neural pathways. Powerful experiences, including powerful religious experiences, actually lead the brain to "rewire" itself in new ways. The point for us is a simple one: when we have experiences of faith, they can literally change our minds.

Faith: Living a Spiritual Life

VIRTUAL CHURCH

Branston and Monika sit next to one another in an Internet programming course at the community college. Bored with the ramblings of the teacher, Monika notices that Branston is reading a web site operated by a television evangelist.

Monika: Are you into that sort of thing?

Branston: Are you kidding? I was looking for something else and came across this page. Look at this horse hockey about the end of the world. I'm always amazed at the weird things people believe.

Monika: My aunt gives money to that group.

Branston: Really? All she's doing is helping them buy themselves Cadillacs and big white hairdos. Haven't you tried to stop her?

Monika: No, she likes the program. She knows everyone on it by name and likes to talk about the things they do and say on the show. She gets comfort from it, and she lives alone, so who cares?

Branston: I think these people are criminals. They teach people that they can get a miracle if they send in their money and put a piece of wood from Jerusalem in their pockets.

Monika: All I know is that she is lonely. Once they even read a letter from her on the air and prayed for her hip to get better.

Branston: Did it ever get better?

Monika: She says it did.

JOHN'S TRADITION

It turns out that the Jesus who pushes the difference between faith and belief is chiefly found in the Gospels of Matthew, Mark, and Luke, which share much in common. But the Gospel of John apparently drew from a different collection or tradition of stories of

SMALL GROUP

Virtual Church

Read the dialogue between Monika and Branston. Discuss these questions in your small group:

Do you think Monika's aunt should be stopped from giving to the television evangelist? Why or why not? Does it make any difference whether her aunt actually experienced healing or only thought she did? Do people have to believe in the "right thing" to experience a miracle? Or do you think the mind is so powerful that if you believe something hard enough you can be healed? Are all miracles from God? Explain.

DISCUSS

John's Tradition

How would you describe the difference in experience between having faith (noun) and believing (verb), and between having knowledge and knowing?

Faith as Knowledge of Jesus

Examine the whole context of this story by reading John 6:41-69. John's Gospel does not include the story of Jesus initiating the practice of Holy Communion (Matthew 26:26-29; Mark 14:22-25; Luke 22:14-20). But all of this talk about eating Jesus' flesh and drinking his blood refers to Communion. Note in the text the difficulty that this kind of language apparently caused in the early days of Christianity. How do you personally experience this language about eating flesh and drinking blood? What deeper truths does it try to convey? Should the fact that it is offensive for some be a concern for the church? Or should its strangeness be valued and preserved?

Signposts

SMALL GROUP

Break into groups of two people. Let each group choose to read and discuss one of the seven miraculous signs. It doesn't matter if some of the signs get left out of the process. Try to identify the symbolic role that the sign may play by examining the discourse that surrounds it or immediately follows it. It may help to compare your sign to the "I am" statements listed in Biblical Studies 101 on page 64. How does this sign illuminate the identity of Jesus in John? How do you personally understand that identity description?

Jesus and in many ways has a very different theological viewpoint from the others.

In John, for example, the noun for "faith" (*pistis*) never appears, although it appears two hundred forty-three times in the rest of the New Testament. John prefers action words like *believing* and *knowing* (*knowledge* never appears in John either). To put it another way, for John, faith and knowledge are not things you *have*, but things you *do*.

In fact, believing and knowing are so closely related that they are one and the same thing in this Gospel. For John believing or knowing is always directed *into* something—God, the name of Jesus, and Jesus himself. So true knowledge and true belief for John means knowledge of and belief in Jesus (or the God revealed by Jesus).

Read John 6:66-69.

Jesus started teaching that he was the "bread of heaven" and that his disciples would have to eat his flesh and drink his blood. (Back up to 6:41-65 to get the whole scene.) Not surprisingly, upon hearing these strange words, many of the people who were following Jesus dropped out. Jesus, turning to the twelve core disciples, then asked them if they wanted to flee too. Peter's words are telling and representative of the sort of response John wants to coax from his readers: "Lord, to whom can we go? You have the words of eternal life. We have come to [*believe*] and [*know*] that you are the Holy One of God" (6:68-69).

Clearly the disciples exemplify John's connection of belief and knowledge, faith and brain. Their *experience* of Jesus has rewired their brains to *think* of Jesus in a new way. And what was that experience? In John, Jesus is experienced as the one who gives signs.

SIGNPOSTS

Another striking difference between John and the other Gospels is how they treat the miracles Jesus performs. Matthew, Mark, and Luke are all dominated by Jesus' miracles. But John reports only seven miraculous "signs," all of which occur in the first half of the book:

- turning water into wine at the wedding feast (John 2:1-11);
- healing the official's son in Cana (4:46-54);
- healing the ill man at the pool of Bethzatha (5:1-18);
- feeding the five thousand (6:1-15);
- walking on the sea (6:16-21);
- healing the man born blind (9:1-41);
- raising Lazarus from the dead (11:17-44).

There are no exorcisms here and no signs or miracles in the second half of the Gospel at all (Chapters 12–21, excluding the Resurrection and post-Resurrection stories, of course).

The signs themselves are mostly symbolic in meaning, as indicated by the long discourses that generally follow. They are not included by John just to describe Jesus as a miracle-worker, but to point to Jesus' identity as the Son of God. The signs are guideposts to believing in and knowing Jesus.

FOUR RESPONSES

But like all signs, human beings have different reactions to them. Think of a typical "Stay Off the Grass" sign, for example. There are at least four different ways that this sign can engage the brains of the people who pass by it:

Closer Look
Take one or more of the seven "I am" statements listed in the Biblical Studies 101 box and study it closely. Read the larger context in John where the statement appears. Is it related to one of the seven signs? Using a Bible dictionary or concordance, study the meaning of the image or word that Jesus uses (i.e., bread of life, sheepgate, shepherd, vine). What role did this symbol play in the culture or economy of that time? What religious symbolic role did it play in Judaism? How does this "I am" statement try to make connections between the identity of Jesus and God? In what way is the statement shocking or surprising?

Four Responses
Using the "Stay Off the Grass" sign or a sign of your own choosing, try to add to the list of possible responses we make to signs. Do you obey (or not obey) signs because they are symbols of authority? because they represent accumulated wisdom? What kind of signs are you inclined to obey and what kind do you typically ignore?

Faith as Knowledge of Jesus

Four Responses

Carefully read John 4:46-54; 12:36b-43; 20:19-28, 29-31. If you wish, form four small groups and divide the passages. Take note of the situation, the statements of Jesus, and the response of the characters in the story. Which of the responses to the signs are commended? Which are condemned? How do the four passages combine to persuade us which response we should have? Do you see yourself in these stories anywhere? If so, how? What do they mean for your life now?

Biblical Studies 101: "I AM"

In John, the identity of Jesus is revealed in seven statements that Jesus makes about himself. They are commonly called the "I am" statements, because that's how Jesus began each one.

"I am the bread of life" (6:35, 51).

"I am the light of the world" (8:12).

"I am the gate for the sheep" (10:7).

"I am the good shepherd" (10:11).

"I am the resurrection and the life" (11:25).

"I am the way, and the truth, and the life" (14:6).

"I am the true vine" (15:1).

Here and elsewhere in the Gospel, Jesus used a form of "I am" that was understood as one of the divine names of God (see Biblical Studies 101: YHWH on page 38 about God's name). So Jesus is being quite literal when he says, "I have come in my Father's name" (5:43) and "The Father and I are one" (10:30).

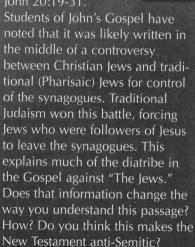

Closer Look

Look more closely at John 20:19-31.

Students of John's Gospel have noted that it was likely written in the middle of a controversy between Christian Jews and traditional (Pharisaic) Jews for control of the synagogues. Traditional Judaism won this battle, forcing Jews who were followers of Jesus to leave the synagogues. This explains much of the diatribe in the Gospel against "The Jews." Does that information change the way you understand this passage? How? Do you think this makes the New Testament anti-Semitic?

1. One person who was tempted to walk on the grass sees the sign, takes it seriously, and decides to stay on the sidewalk.
2. Another sees the sign but thinks it won't do any harm if just one person walks on the grass.
3. Another walks by the sign without noticing it and walks on the grass.
4. Yet another doesn't see the sign but notices that the grass is freshly sown and knows to stay off.

The same pattern can be observed in John's Gospel.

Read John 4:46-54.

A royal official comes to Jesus to ask him to heal his son. Although Jesus agrees, and heals him with a spoken word and at a long distance, he doesn't do so before making an observation about this man's faith: "Unless

64

you see signs and wonders you will not believe." Many of us are like this. We believe that there are signposts to God in this world but will not have faith unless we see some ourselves.

Read John 12:36b-43.

Jesus is frustrated by the lack of understanding of the crowd in Jerusalem. Although they had witnessed many of the signs, they did not make the mental connection between what they saw and what they believed about Jesus. Notice how the voice of John the narrator here interrupts the story with a severe judgment that draws from the prophet Isaiah. Hardened hearts, spiritual blindness, and fear of losing one's social standing are all reasons named for denying the meaning of the signs.

Read John 20:19-28.

Thomas missed the sign of Jesus' resurrection because he happened to be absent. Although he had the testimony of his friends and colleagues he was adamant: "Unless I see and touch, I will not believe." It is not really fair to call him "doubting" Thomas, for when Jesus does come again, all it takes is one glance (Thomas never really touched Jesus), and he is a believer. But he is not just one who believes the sign; he presses through to a deeper meaning: what the sign says about the identity of Jesus.

Read John 20:29-31.

Jesus gently chides Thomas for his literal-mindedness. In doing so, he blesses all of those who come to belief even though they don't see. Of course that's the position that all of us who live after Jesus are in: having to choose to believe or not to believe in Jesus without having seen him or his signs.

Do you think Thomas's demand to see and to touch is understandable or childish? expected? typical? strange? Why? Do you identify with his skepticism? What difference does that make in how you engage your faith? Note again how the voice of John the narrator intrudes, this time turning its attention directly to *you*, the reader. How does it make you feel to be addressed like that?

Should religion always be rational? Should Christianity always be rational? Why or why not? St. Anselm, a famous theologian, talked about the importance of "faith seeking understanding." Our brains are divided into two halves: the left lobe specializes in logical, rational, and word-oriented thought, while the right specializes in creative, associative, and artistic thought. Are these equally important to the life of faith? Does our post-modern age tend to value or need one more than the other? Why? Do you experience your faith primarily from one side? What strengths and weaknesses does this present?

Faith as Knowledge of Jesus

But is this rational? Is it reasonable to ask us to hitch our faith to a Jesus we have never actually seen? John clearly thought so, and that's why he wrote his Gospel. Although he had other signs from which to choose (John 21:25), he very deliberately related these signs so that those who read the story would believe in him.

He hoped that our brains would make the connection between what we experienced in the reading and what we believe. His goal was to write down the story of Jesus in such a way that it would rewire not only our brains, but our entire lives, "so that you may come to believe that Jesus is the Messiah, the Son of God, and that through believing you may have life in his name" (20:31).

FUSING THE WORD WITH MY WORLD

John's Gospel is a literary masterpiece. It summons the best evidence and testimony it can about Jesus and fashions it carefully to lead its readers to a specific conclusion. But does it work?

Deep faith in Jesus probably won't come from reading one testimony, even if it is the beautiful and persuasive prose of John. Those mental connections between mature faith and belief require years of action, reflection, reading, struggling, and community. But mental connections can and must be established between our faith and our brains if faith is to endure and help us make sense of our world. It is hard work. Life "in his name" is adventure travel, not a luxury tour.

TRADITION

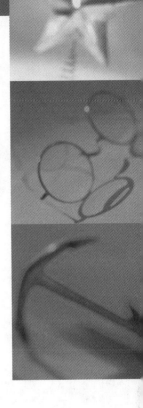

This session explores the link between faith traditions and contemporary lives.

THE CHRISTIAN CULT

A sociologist of religion in the Roman Empire would have described early Christianity as a cult. Like the Mormons in the nineteenth century and the "Moonies" in the twentieth, the Christian movement emerged in its time as something that seemed strange or even deviant to others.

Its members, as one contemporary sociologist has argued, were chiefly drawn from the ranks of middle or upper-middle class Jews who lived in the overcrowded Greek cities of the Empire, like Ephesus, Antioch, and Corinth. Looking for a religion that retained much of their Jewish heritage but better helped them cope with being ethnic minorities in the predominant Greco-Roman culture, they were attracted to the liberating message contained in the gospel (good news) of Jesus. One can easily imagine concerned Jewish parents in Antioch throwing up their hands in despair when one of their children became a Christian, and asking one another: "Where did we go wrong?"

Getting Started
Using a chalkboard or a piece of poster paper, write down a list of as many cults as you can think of. Then make a list of things that characterize cults. Ask: Why do people find them threatening?

Converts to this cult were easily identifiable. They:

- knit themselves together in close communities;
- held much of their property in common and shared it as each had need;
- conducted secret rituals in members' homes rumored to involve the drinking of blood and the eating of flesh;
- refused to participate in Roman civil religion (worship of the emperor and the pagan gods);
- shared strange books of writings among themselves;
- accepted women as leaders in their communities;
- tended the sick and the poor during natural disasters and epidemics;
- practiced strict moral rules, particularly in the area of sexuality and birth control.

All these things set them apart from the predominant culture and gave members their own clear identity, their own sense of belonging. The demands placed upon followers of Jesus in those early years were such that one did not join the movement casually nor leave it quickly when there were disagreements or difficulties. When threatened by the Roman authorities, as they were occasionally, Christians showed a frustrating obstinacy in their religious beliefs, even preferring death to the betrayal of their friends.

AN INHERITED FAITH

By the second or third generation after Jesus, what had begun as a rather loose Jewish reform movement began to solidify into its own identity, taking on many of the

SMALL

GROUP

The Christian Cult
Break into small groups and ask one another: Have you or anyone in your family ever been in conflict with your parents or other parental figures over your religious beliefs or practices? If so, what were the circumstances? Did this get resolved or is it an ongoing area of conflict?

Do you perceive your church as something that is easy to join and leave or as something with fairly strong boundaries? What difference does the way it defines its boundaries make to its experience of community? Is your faith something for which you would be willing to suffer or die? Why or why not?

characteristics of a separate cult, even a separate religion. Besides the things already mentioned, this involved the regularization of leadership roles into distinct offices like bishop (overseer) and deacon (servant or attendant). It also involved the regularization of the *content* of the Christian faith. The rather informal message of and about Jesus fairly quickly became a "deposit" of faith—a tradition handed down from one generation to another.

Read 2 Timothy 1:1-7.

Many of the "books" of the New Testament are really letters, of course. The three letters of First and Second Timothy and Titus are often described as the "pastoral" epistles of Paul because they seem to be letters written from one Christian leader or "pastor" to another.

Here we have the opening words of a rather personal letter to Paul's prodigy, Timothy. It was written, probably from Ephesus, to a trusted person who had responsibility over several churches. Paul noted that the faith Timothy has "lived first in your grandmother Lois and your mother Eunice" (1:5). He received his faith as a gift, not only from them but from Paul himself, who calls him, "my beloved child" (1:2). Paul acted as Timothy's mentor and commissioned him for leadership by the ritual of "laying on of hands" (1:6). This gift of faith and leadership is what Paul wants Timothy to "rekindle" within him as he faces a serious conflict in his churches.

Later in this letter, Paul admonished Timothy not to waver in the faith he inherited from his mentors and from the Jewish tradition: "But as for you, continue in what you have learned and firmly believed, knowing from whom you learned it, and how from childhood you have known the sacred writings [the Hebrew Bible or Old

SMALL GROUP

An Inherited Faith

Ask one another to relate the formative influences on their own religious lives. What kind of faith did your grandparents have? your parents? Do you feel as if you have inherited a faith tradition or are you making it up as you go along? What benefits and costs have there been for you in this?

BIBLE

Read 2 Timothy 1:1-7.

Now look at the closing of the letter in 4:19-22. Compare the opening and closing of this letter with the other pastoral epistles of First Timothy and Titus. If you want to go further, compare them with the openings and closings for some of the other letters in the New Testament, like Romans, Galatians, and First and Second Thessalonians. Discuss: What themes recur in these opening and closing sections? To whom and how are they addressed? What indications do you see that these letters were mostly dictated to a secretary? Why do you think these letters were an effective "technology" for helping the early church to grow? Would such letters be effective today? Why or why not?

Closer Look
Learn more about the conflict Timothy faced by reading 2 Timothy 2:14-19. At least two persons, Hymenaeus and Philetus, had introduced new teachings to the congregation. Use a Bible dictionary or commentary to find out more about these persons and about the problem.

Paul saw himself as a mentor for Timothy. Have you ever had a mentor? a religious mentor? Who? How did he or she influence your life?

Read 2 Timothy 3:10-17 for a closer look at Paul's mentoring activity with Timothy.

Testament] that are able to instruct you for salvation through faith in Christ Jesus" (2 Timothy 3:14-15).

A COMMON FAITH

Read Titus 1:1-4.

Titus is another of the pastoral epistles, a letter written by Paul (or by a disciple of Paul writing in his name), to another leader in the church. As in Timothy, Paul speaks affectionately of Titus, describing him as "my loyal child in the faith we share" (1:4; 1 Timothy 1:2).

Read Titus 1:1-4 again. Note how the word *faith* has now come to mean something that people hold in common, something they share. Paul portrays himself now as the guardian of a set of beliefs about Jesus (1:3; 2 Timothy 1:12), that are to be passed on to others. Here we see a definite sign that the loose movement of Jesus' followers is turning into a cult with specific beliefs. The church is becoming an institution.

To make this shift clearer, recall that the noun for *faith* (*pistis*) never appeared in John's Gospel, which preferred the action words of *knowing* and *believing* (Session 6). Similarly, for most of the Hebrew Bible, and for the Jesus portrayed in Matthew, Mark, and Luke, faith is mostly a matter of *trust* in God (Session 2). For the writer of Hebrews, faith is a matter of *hope* for God's

future (Session 1). These are all relatively dynamic understandings of faith.

But here faith has become a body of beliefs that must be taught carefully to future generations and guarded from alternative views. The Jesus movement is now Christianity. Faith in Christ is now *"the* faith."

KEEP OUT THE INTRUDERS!

These pastoral epistles, and indeed many of the writings of the New Testament, were deeply concerned with stamping out false teachings about Jesus. A sentence from First Timothy is a great example of this fear of doctrinal pollution:

"Now the Spirit expressly says that in later times some will renounce the faith by paying attention to deceitful spirits and teachings of demons, through the hypocrisy of liars whose consciences are seared with a hot iron" (4:1-2).

Or as the brief letter of Jude states:

"Beloved . . . I find it necessary to write and appeal to you to contend for the faith that was once for all entrusted to the saints. For certain intruders have stolen in among you. . ." (3-4).

Such language recalls Jesus' distinction between the good shepherd who knows the sheep by name and protects them from wolves, and the hired hand who "sees the wolf coming and leaves the sheep and runs away" (John 10:12).

What is clear from these passages and the many others like them in the New Testament, was that the early Christians did indeed feel marginalized and threatened by their surrounding culture. Their religious identity was newly born and vulnerable to outside influences. Their careful safeguarding, boundary-keeping, teaching,

A Common Faith

Do you think that this shift in meaning for faith into a "body of beliefs" is a decline from the earlier meanings or a natural and necessary occurrence? One theologian has wryly said that Jesus promised the kingdom of God and we got the church instead. Do you think Jesus meant to found a new religion? Why or why not? Can one be a follower of Jesus and not be a member of the Christian faith? Why or why not?

Keep Out the Intruders!

Read 1 Timothy 4:1-2, and Titus 3-4. What do these warnings tell you about the life of the early faith community? Do you see any evidence of the church today trying to "stamp out false teaching?" What forms does that take? Is it effective? Can you think of any instances in the past when the church tried to stamp out something in a way we now regret? Are there any "false teachings" that you are concerned about today? What measures should the church take to separate themselves from them? How confident can it be that it is making the right decision? Why?

and admonishing were ways to protect their faith and pass it on to future generations.

SMALL GROUP

Religious Sclerosis?
Break into small groups and take one of the three questions listed here. Take some time to explore the meaning of the question and come up with some possible answers. If desired, have your small groups report their findings to the larger group.

DISCUSS

Refer to "The Visit" on page 76. In addition to the questions in the case study, ask: Some would consider the visitors intruders. How would you regard them? Some religions that Christians consider false also send out missionaries or evangelists. How can you tell when "intruders have stolen in among you"?

RELIGIOUS SCLEROSIS?

In some ways this trend was also a loss for the dynamic Jesus movement, a hardening of the spiritual arteries. Most renewal movements in Christianity have tried to recapture some of the early dynamism that they feel has been eclipsed by the church institution and its formal worship style. Inevitably, if these renewal movements survive, they go through the same process of solidification that the early church went through: naming leaders, drawing boundaries, excluding heretics. But that the church of Jesus continues to thrive throughout the world today is testimony to its early efforts to set limits.

This trend from movement to cult to institution also begs some key questions of us as we near the end of this study of faith:

- Is there a pure kind of faith outside a community of defined belief?
- How does our faith get shaped by the groups we join? the church or tradition we inherit from our families?
- What is the benefit or cost to us as we "shop around" for a religious tradition, denomination, or church that suits us?

PRAYING ALONE

Very generally speaking, those of us raised in the Protestant (non-Roman Catholic or Eastern Orthodox) culture have been taught that faith is predominantly an individual (even private) matter. This way of thinking is so pervasive in our culture

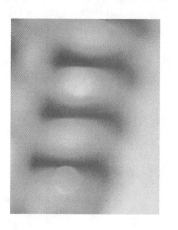

that we fail to see just how heavily we all have been shaped by it, whether we are fundamentalist Christians or New Age seekers. Here are some general characteristics of this individualistic way of thinking:

- a distrust of anyone who claims to be a religious authority. All persons are thought to have equal access to religious truths;
- an emphasis on personal religious experience or feeling;
- a distrust of or lack of interest in anything that seems formal or ritualistic in worship;
- an expectation or hope of sudden or quick conversions rather than life-long struggles of change;
- a lack of interest in or a suspicion of religious tradition;
- an aversion to hearing from others how much to pray, how much money to give, or how often to attend worship;
- a conviction that it is perfectly natural and ordinary for people to change religious affiliations as they see fit, to church-shop, drive for miles to go to a church they prefer rather than the one around the corner, or to join or to leave a congregation when there is a change in pastors or a personal disagreement.

In Europe, Asia, and most other places in the world, the idea of switching religions or denominations is rare and seems strange. In our culture it has become the norm.

FUSING THE WORD WITH MY WORLD

Early Christians did not join the Jesus cult lightly because the social stigma was high and the changes it wrought on one's life were severe. Nonetheless, the group

Praying Alone

How many of these traits of individualism do your recognize as operating in your own spiritual life or in your church community?

Using a chalkboard or a piece of poster paper, try to come up with an acceptable alternative view for each of the characteristics listed here. For example, a positive alternative to our distrust of religious authorities might be: "A trust of those whose lives reflect the deep wisdom of a religious tradition."

Note: This may prove a difficult exercise. You may want to try only a few of these. Do not rush the process.

Fusing the Word With My World

What does the statement, "Jesus Christ expected so much of them," mean to you? How can this be reconciled to something that Jesus says in Matthew 11:29-30: "Take my yoke upon you, and learn from me; for my yoke is easy and my burden is light."
Do you think of yourself as "belonging" to a church? denomination? religious tradition? Why or why not?

Are there any traditions that you think are being born or are dying in our own day? What are they? Why are they changing like this?

Closing
Light a candle if desired. Recall aloud the images of faith that we have thought about together, faith as

- hope
- confidence
- trust
- salvation
- good works
- knowledge of Jesus
- tradition

Going around the room, identify which of these images seem most important to you in your life with God today. Perhaps you will choose an image that seemed new and interesting, or one that represents your own understanding of faith most closely. If you want, you can simply name it. Or, you may choose to briefly explain your reason for choosing it to the other members.

Close using this prayer:

"God of grace,
You shared your life with us in the person of Jesus and entrusted us with a measure of faith. Inspire our hearts, that having the courage to witness to this gift of faith, our lives might begin to reflect the great love you have for us and for the whole of your creation, through Jesus Christ. Amen."

End by passing the peace.

grew at a steady pace. And within about three hundred years it had grown so large that with the help of Emperor Constantine (d. 337), it dominated the Roman Empire. People accepted what was now called *the* faith (or the religion) of Christianity not only because they thought it was true, but because the rewards were so great. They became members of a new family in which they were well treated and challenged to grow in their faith and serve others in love. People were attracted to Jesus Christ precisely because he expected so much of them.

In our everyday language, it is not uncommon for us to ask someone: "What religion (or denomination) do you belong to?" To belong to something means that you are somehow "owned" by it. That's a difficult concept for us individualists. But however much we think of ourselves as on our own journeys of faith, we have inherited and benefited by a rich tradition of faithfulness that came before us. Not everything about our traditions should be honored or kept. Traditions themselves are born and die over the course of the centuries. But as faithful people ourselves, we link our lives with those that came before us so that we can offer our best understanding of God to those who will come after us. Paul put it nicely to Timothy:

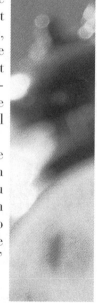

"You then, my child, be strong in the grace that is in Christ Jesus; and what you have heard from me through many witnesses entrust to faithful people who will be able to teach others as well" (2 Timothy 2:1-2).

CASE STUDIES

Getting Started

Use any of these case studies throughout your *Faith* study to enhance the lesson and to dig deeper into issues of faith.

What's the Use?

Terri is very frustrated. Work is a huge hassle, mainly due to a new and very clueless boss. Terri confided to Jeff, a Christian friend at work, what a difficulty it is in the morning getting motivated to come in to the office. When he suggested she look for a new job, that wasn't a satisfying option either. Then Jeff confronted Terri about why she was reluctant to leave her job if it was so miserable.

"It's not the job that's the problem," she said. "I think the work I do is important. It offers something helpful and necessary to others, and I feel like I'm a part of a bigger, meaningful picture. I think this is my calling, a way to express my Christian faith. It's just the environment and working conditions that are the pain."

"Well, have you prayed about it?"

"Sort of," she confessed. "But God knows what the problem is without my having to report on it, and this boss seems pretty content to stay. So what good would prayer do? What's going to change if I pray?"

- Is this a faith issue? If so, what makes it so?

- For what could Terri trust God in this situation? What does she seem to trust in now?

- What is the relationship, in Terri's mind, between prayer and God's response?

- If you were Jeff what might you suggest next to Terri?

- What does Terri understand the purpose of prayer to be? If you were Terri, how would you word your prayer about this situation? For whom or what would you pray? Why? What is the role of prayer for you in establishing and maintaining your own relationship with God?

The Visit

Ty took the day off to do some chores around the house. Just after lunch, the doorbell rang and there stood two well-groomed young men in suits with their Bibles. After a quick debate about whether to invite them in, Ty thought, *Why not? I'll have some fun with these guys. This religion stuff is silly. A good debate will show them a thing or two.*

The two men opened their conversation with some form of "Brother, are you saved?" and the debate was on. To his surprise Ty found their conversation made sense to him. For every argument he presented, they found Scripture to challenge him. By the time they left, his head was spinning, especially when he heard himself say that he would be glad to see them again.

A week later, they returned, this time just after dinner. Ty could tell his wife was not at all interested in entertaining, so he talked to them alone for about two hours. When they asked him to open his heart and accept Christ in his life, he did. The visitors had not been gone ten minutes before Ty's wife was ridiculing him for "getting religion."

What issues of faith do you see here?

■ What do you think of this conversion story? Do you think Ty's conversion is a temporary or permanent part of his life of faith? Why? What should he do from this point forward to grow his faith?

■ Have you ever been in a situation where your belief or faith system was turned upside down? What did that feel like? What happened? What did you do?

■ What would be your reaction if these two men knocked on your door? What assumptions do you make about them beyond what is mentioned in the story above? Why? What further role should or could the two visitors play in Ty's next steps in faith?

■ What might be going on in the mind of Ty's wife? When one partner undergoes a radical religious conversion, what are the implications for family or significant friends?

■ As a Christian who works with Ty, what might you do when he talks about this experience with you? if he was converted by persons whose denomination or faith orientation is very different from yours? by methods with which you may be uncomfortable?

The Viewing

Tamika and Tommy are in shock and grief. Tommy's eighty-two-year-old grandmother was caring for their toddler. She had taken him with her on a brief trip to the grocery store when a drunk driver collided with them and killed them instantly.

Now, at the viewing at the funeral home, scores of family, friends, neighbors, and coworkers are offering whatever words of comfort they can and are struggling to find meaning in this tragedy. In two hours they have heard these comments and more.

"God will take care of everything. Just trust in God."

"That driver will be judged for what she did to destroy your family."

"I'm so sorry this has happened. I'll keep you in my prayers."

"Don't try to guess God's motives. Whatever happens is God's will; God knows best."

"God doesn't cause tragedy, sin does. This is not God's doing, but God will take care of you."

"It must have been your grandmother's time, and God will give you another child. Everything will be ok."

"You shouldn't be angry with God; that's a sin."

"It's okay to be angry with God for letting this happen. Bad things happen to faithful people. God is big enough to handle your feelings and see you through this painful time."

"Call me anytime I can be of help. I'll coordinate with all the folks at church if you need anything at all."

All of these are faith statements.

■ Which statements seem to you to build up and encourage? Why?

■ Which seem less than helpful? Why?

■ Have you said anything similar to these comments in a situation of grief? What did you mean by it and what did you intend to convey?

■ What do these statements say about God? about the speaker's trust, faith, and belief about God?

■ If you were Tommy or Tamika, how would you be feeling?

■ What words of faith would you offer them? What actions of faith would you offer?

The "Cross to Bear"

Doña Amanda has two young adult daughters and a severe case of rheumatoid arthritis that severely limits her range of motion, strength, and flexibility. She needs a lot of help around the house. Both of her daughters, Carmen and Lia, live fairly close by, so one or the other is usually available to give assistance, at least after work. Lia is just like her mother, which in this case means that they don't get along very well. Carmen's relationship is much more compatible with her mother, and she and her sister Lia are close as well.

Because Doña Amanda picks at Lia and because they tend to bicker, Lia resents having to spend a lot of time with her mother. She does what she can, and with as much care as possible, but it always feels like torture. Lia refers to it as her "cross to bear."

Carmen loves her sister, but this martyr-like response gets to her. She loves helping out and also finds time to spend unrelated to the chores her mother needs done. On the other hand, Carmen generally makes a point to her sister about how much Doña Amanda appreciates what she does and what a blessing it is to be able to help and serve such a wonderful mother. Doña Amanda is always giving Carmen little "rewards" for being so good to her.

■ What are the faith issues here?

■ Both daughters believe their service to their mother is rooted in their faith, but they look at it very differently. Can they both be right? Explain.

■ Can Lia's service rendered grudgingly be considered faithful? Why or why not?

■ If Carmen helps out with an eye to the rewards, is her service faithful? Explain.

■ How are Carmen and Lia being faithful (or not) to each other?

SERVICE LEARNING OPTIONS

Consider trying one or more of these service options as a way to put your faith into action.

IDEA #1: Plan an interreligious service.

With others in your group, and with the help of your pastor, plan either to attend a worship service of another denomination or of a congregation that is theologically different from your own stance. To gain more than just a "tourist's" view, plan to attend at least three times so that you see the patterns of worship and style more clearly and get a more personal feel for the members. Then take the next steps to invite those members into dialog to explore common and diverse interests and beliefs, and if possible, plan for cooperative ministries.

IDEA #2: Plan for and engage in a ministry of witness or advocacy in which you share and act out what you really believe. If you want to start more modestly, place yourself in a position in which you at least have to be firm about what you believe, even if you are not ready to reach out with it. Some arenas of service include tutoring in an after-school program at a community church; joining the evangelism team in your congregation; teaching a Bible study; joining or forming a prayer group or prayer chain with like-minded persons at church or work; offering "fix-it" assistance to older adults in your community; working with prisoners for job training, in Bible study, in remedial social skills; helping in an adult literacy program; or working with voter registration drives.

IDEA #3: Hold a love feast to conclude your study.

Find a quiet room in which you will be undisturbed. Have water and good quality, unsliced baker's bread on hand (or have a covered-dish dinner instead).

Begin your time with a hymn or song followed by a prayer of thanksgiving for the group and for your time together. Read aloud a Scripture passage (such as Psalm 145; 1 Corinthians 13; Philippians 2:5-11; 1 John 4:7-21; Luke 14:16-24; John 6:25-35).

The bread and water or meal is then shared. Participants can offer food to one another as a sign of community and love, but it should not be served as Communion.

During the time of eating and sharing, members of the group can offer informal testimonies of faith, speaking clearly and directly of how they perceive God working in their lives and in the lives of those around them. It is appropriate to mention particular prayer concerns or thanksgivings as well.

When the testimonies reach a natural ending point, close with a psalm or a prayer and the passing of the peace.